Five Speeches That Changed the World

FIVE SPEECHES THAT CHANGED THE WORLD

Ben F. Meyer

A Liturgical Press Book

THE LITURGICAL PRESS
Collegeville, Minnesota

COVER DESIGN: Ann Blattner. ILLUSTRATION: Sermon on the Mount, from *Das Leben: 33 Scherenschnitte von Melchior Grossek* (Freiburg im Breisgau: Herder, 1923).

Printed in the United States of America.

Library of Congress Cataloging-in-Publication Data

Meyer, Ben F., 1927–
    Five speeches that changed the world / Ben F. Meyer.
        p.   cm.
    Includes bibliographical references.
    ISBN 0-8146-2282-8
    1. Bible. N.T. Matthew—Criticism, interpretation, etc.
I. Title. II. Title: 5 speeches that changed the world.
BS2575.2.M49 1994
226.2'06—dc20   93-43726
                                              CIP

pour l'unique

DIONISAKI

CONTENTS

PREFACE

This effort to present anew the five speeches in the Gospel of Matthew includes an attempt to translate them anew. To be sure, the translations are not altogether original. I have drawn on the Revised Standard Version and other English-language versions (e.g., the Revised English Bible), as well as on Paul Joüon's *L'Evangile de Notre-Seigneur Jésus-Christ* (Paris: Beauchesne, 1930) and the scholarly work of Gustaf Dalman and Joachim Jeremias.

Words for which there is an entry in the Glossary are preceded by an asterisk (e.g., *Sitz im Leben*, *School of Alexandria) the first time they appear. Also at the end of the book are a few endnotes giving bibliographical data.

BEN F. MEYER

Les Verrières, Switzerland
August 1992

INTRODUCTION

The five speeches from the Gospel according to Matthew that are the subject of this book not only changed the world but are still changing it. No other speeches in human history have had as great an impact as these five have had. What speech could rank with the Sermon on the Mount for its influence on the hearts of men and women throughout the centuries? One thinks first of the peerless humanism and cool, long-term confidence that shine through the speech of Pericles during the Peloponnesian War; of the Apology of Socrates, with its shifts of tone from simplicity and modesty to its notes of tough-minded challenge issued by a man unafraid of death; of the passionate but futile Philippics of Demosthenes. Or one might think of the speeches of Cicero, passages of which generations of schoolchildren from the Renaissance to the time of our parents more or less profitably learned by heart.

Then there is the series of eloquent discourses that Moses delivered as the children of Israel were poised to cross the Jordan River into the land of Canaan. Contained in the Book of Deuteronomy, these speeches are marked by a compelling rhetoric of thanks and fear and love, and rank as the greatest in the Old Testament.

How about the Fire Sermon of the Buddha? A striking speech, but it has had no *liturgical* role comparable to that of Jesus' speeches in Christian liturgy. And this is the cardinal, though not the deepest, secret of the historic phenomenon of these "five speeches that changed the world." Liturgy is the hinge: the speeches of Jesus in the Gospel of Matthew have had and still have a living *Sitz im Leben*, that is, a recurrent

11

social context for the repetition of a text, in the life of Christianity. These speeches are still read out today, just as they have been all through the life of Christianity in unbroken continuity from the end of the first century. No other speeches known to humankind have been repeated more regularly over the centuries than those of Jesus as found in Matthew's Gospel.

One might urge the claims of the farewell speech of Jesus to his disciples in chapters 13–17 of the Gospel of John. But when the shapers of the Christian liturgy in the third, fourth, and fifth centuries went about their task (and it is their work that has been decisive), they considered the Gospel of John to be one of the texts for which the catechumens were not yet ready.

Again, one might argue for the claims of the Gospel of Luke, with its pungent opening speech on love for enemies (the Sermon on the Plain) and its unique apocalyptic speech in chapter 17 telling the disciples about how "the day of the Son of Man" would come (a key to Jesus' view of the future).

The fact is that those who shaped the liturgy preferred Matthew, the most effective of the primitive Christian catechists. And there is a sense in which the heart of his catechesis was the five great speeches that strategically mark off his whole great Gospel like a series of surveyor's pickets.

In substance these five speeches, the present writer is convinced, derive from Jesus, despite our not knowing with any precision how much of the material already had a "discourse structure" in its earliest form, close to the memory of Jesus. Historical and comparative analyses are of some help at this point. It is unlikely that Jesus ever gave a speech made up entirely of parables. Something similar can be said of the speech on the Church in Matthew 18. In a word, the third and fourth of Jesus' five speeches in Matthew's Gospel were not speeches at all originally. When we say that all five "derived" from Jesus, we mean that he provided the substance of the material later organized in speech form.

Our analysis of Jesus' speeches, though it will often deal incidentally with aspects of research about the historical Jesus, is not directly and primarily a study of the historical Jesus. It is a study of Jesus as he and his words have come down to us, first through the processes of oral tradition and, eventually, through the Gospel literature. But it should be said from the start that the refractions of oral tradition and the stylizing of literary Gospels have by no means given us a fictional, non-historical Jesus. In Matthew we are in touch with the Jesus who *was*—and who, as Christian faith affirms, *still is* and, as the last words of Matthew's Gospel say, *will be*, and will be *with us*, "even to the end of the age."

Five Speeches That Changed the World is meant for a wide readership. It is not a piece of scholarship deliberately limited to scholars; but neither is it an effort by an outsider to biblical scholarship. Even the best of the outsiders—Frank Kermode and Northrop Frye—were drawn to the Bible to test their already formulated literary theories. Unhappily, as guides to the Bible they are regularly misleading. Perhaps they underrated the specific traits of biblical literature. Their efforts are not unlike the translations of the New Testament that have come from classical scholars who underrated the disadvantage of not being at home either in the *Koine Greek of the writers or in the environmental research relevant to the texts. ("I am the beautiful shepherd," reads John 10:11 in the version of E. V. Rieu.) Nor is the present book a secular, religiously neutral work, a solidly established position in biblical scholarship today; much less is it an irreligious or anti-religious effort, like the works of John Allegro or Morton Smith on Jesus, for example.

We would like to avoid as far as possible the jargon and illiteracies (mostly oddities of German-English like "over against" = *gegenüber*) hardly found outside professional biblical scholarship. Where the jargon is so useful as to be irresistible (we have already used *Sitz im Leben*), we shall at least provide a glossary for convenience.

Since the five speeches that changed the world are Matthean, they must be set from the start, even if briefly, in the context of Matthew's Gospel.

Chapter 1

THE GOSPEL OF MATTHEW

Who Matthew was we do not know. There was a Matthew who belonged to the inner circle of Jesus' disciples, one of the Twelve; and in the Markan tradition there was a story of the conversion of Levi, a publican (i.e., a toll-collector), who became a disciple of Jesus.

Now the editor of the Greek Gospel attributed to Matthew took it that Jesus had twelve disciples (Matt 10:1: "and he called to him his twelve disciples"). Levi, according to Mark, was a disciple of Jesus, but the name Levi did not figure in the list of the Twelve. So, in taking over the story of Levi's conversion (Mark 2:13-18), the editor, for the sake of consistency, may have dropped the name Levi and picked another name that *did* show up in the list of the Twelve—Matthew. Thus, perhaps, was born the tradition, not otherwise independently attested, of "Matthew, the publican."[1]

Later still, Christians took this same "Matthew, the publican" to be the author of the Gospel. Why? We do not know, unless it was (a) out of a desire to attribute the Gospel to one of the Twelve, and (b) the only one of the Twelve about whom the author of the Gospel seemed to have special information was Matthew. (The "special information" was that Matthew had been a toll-collector.)

There is, of course, another possibility, namely, that Matthew, one of the Twelve, was the author of the original text that later came down to us much altered and developed, and

15

translated into Greek from "Hebrew" (more probably Aramaic, the language used by Palestinian and other Jews of the time). From internal criticism, however, we have no assurance that the Gospel of Matthew ever existed *as a Gospel* in any language other than Greek.

Who was the author of the *canonical Gospel of Matthew, a Gospel written in Greek, probably in Antioch, and most likely in the period between A.D. 65 and 90? We do not know. Was he Jewish? Perhaps. But if he was, he might well have been an ex-scribe. If so, he was from the prestigious end of the social spectrum, the end opposite that of the rich but outcast toll-collectors.

Current Views

Was there an earlier edition of Matthew's Gospel? On the basis of the testimony of Papias, an early second-century bishop in Western Asia Minor, many have thought so. The following is what Papias says: "Matthew recorded the oracles (*ta logia*) [of Jesus] in the Hebrew tongue and each interpreted them to the best of his ability" (Eusebius, *Church History*, 2.39.16). There could well have been an oral tradition in Aramaic put into writing (by Matthew, one of the Twelve?), which later formed the basis of the canonical Greek version of Matthew. This is one way, but only one way, of filling out what we have from Papias.

Another theory proposes that Matthew, one of the Twelve, provided an original account that served Mark in writing his Gospel and, together with both Mark and a supplementary Synoptic source (largely found paralleled in Luke 9–18), provided the writer of the canonical Gospel of Matthew with the substance of his tradition.

Other theories abound. One that has taken on new life in our time is that the canonical Gospel of Matthew was the first Gospel; Luke rewrote it, producing its counterpart for the Greek-speaking pagan world; and Mark was a synthesis of Matthew and Luke, written to legitimate both.

There is no reason to assume without question that the actual historical relations that obtained among the *Synoptic Gospels as they came into being is a retrievable state of affairs. We do not know for certain whether the history of the *Synoptic tradition and its *redaction in writing were relatively simple or irrecoverably complex. The likelihood of the latter seems at least as good as that of the former. It is therefore perfectly possible that "the *Synoptic question" may designate an insoluble problem.

Our most significant early testimony, that of Luke 1:1-4, suggests that the first forms of the Synoptic tradition derived from Jerusalem, headquarters of Jesus' disciples after his death. But the streams of oral tradition must have crisscrossed variously enough to limit all theorizing on their relations to a sphere ranging from the merely plausible to, at best, some middle-range probability. Whether the Gospel writers copied each other's texts is a question by no means easily settled.

Participants in the enterprise of Synoptic *source criticism seem to be universally persuaded that they are dealing with a problem both solvable and important. Many an outsider (the present writer among them) doubts whether either view is finally viable. It is surprising how little is lost by this selective agnosticism. It merely means that we have no general, systematic solution to the Synoptic problem. It is still possible to operate eclectically, to form particular judgments, for example, on which of two parallel texts is the older. Besides, the pretense of understanding every line of the Gospel text is an old, old mistake. Whereas the main thrust of the meaning of the Synoptic Gospels is available to the attentive reader, there is much that we shall never understand with precision.

The contrary supposition, namely, the claim to comprehensive understanding, has held sway from as early as the patristic *School of Alexandria (third to fifth century). But this supposition, pious and understandable, is surely mistaken. We have plenty of evidence of our ignorance: missing data, irresolvable issues, some small, but others large. Today, in view of the rise of the historical consciousness, the old pretense of comprehensive understanding no longer needs to be sustained, and no longer *can* be sustained. From the eighteenth century to our time, it has become increasingly obsolete.

An example of a problematic issue is "Q," the name given to a hypothetical current of tradition common to Matthew and Luke. The present writer agrees with the *Q hypothesis, but not with the notion that Q began as a written redaction; rather, it was a part of early oral tradition in Aramaic. It was transmitted in at least two forms, translated into Greek, and eventually reached written form, probably first in *"Proto-Luke" or in our Gospels of Matthew and Luke. (A currently favored theory is that Q was a work written in Greek, representing some community's distinctive theology, though elements of it might have circulated in oral tradition, Aramaic or Greek. This view is possible, but mere possibility does not constitute a reason for holding it. As far as the present writer can judge, its positive probability has not been shown.)

It is generally acknowledged that, quite apart from Q, there were narratives in Aramaic drawn on by canonical Matthew. We might call them "M." Whether M was a "gospel" in the full sense is most doubtful. These narratives served the ethos of Jewish-Christian communities in Palestine. In the course of dealing with the five speeches below, we shall have occasion to refer to this stratum of the Matthean tradition.

Our principal effort, and doubtless what is most worth the reader's attention, has little or nothing to do with source-critical theorizing. It is the grasp of the intended meaning of the Matthean text. We shall concentrate on the task of reading this text as exactly as we can.

A clue as to how to go about the task is given by Wystan Hugh Auden. Faced with a text to be interpreted, Auden said there were two questions that interested him. One was technical: Here is a verbal contraption. How does it work? The other was, in a broad sense, moral: What kind of person inhabits this text? What is his idea of the Great Good Place?

These are indeed the questions that count. We shall start with the first one. The effort to find out how this "verbal contraption" works we shall put under the heading "Structure and Style." Then we shall move on to the second question and set it under the heading "Theology."

Structure and Style

The Gospel of Matthew may have reached final form through a minimum of two editions. Whether it did or not, we can hardly know how any previous edition was structured. Hence, of the various structural principles at work in the text of canonical Matthew, we do not know what was inherited and what was contributed by the final *redactor. What we do know is that we have before us in canonical Matthew a diversity of structural principles:

    a) a formal-and-topical structure;
    b) a concentric structure;
    c) a geographical structure;
    d) a theological-and-dramatic structure.

a) *Formal-and-topical structure*

We note first that the Gospel contains five speeches, and that after the infancy narrative and before the story of Jesus' passion and resurrection, narrative and discourse alternate five times:

NARRATIVE 3:1–4:25

DISCOURSE 5:1–7:29   The Sermon on the Mount

NARRATIVE 8:1–10:4

DISCOURSE 10:5–11:1a The Missionary Discourse

NARRATIVE 11:1b–12:50

DISCOURSE 13:1-53a   The Parables Discourse

NARRATIVE 13:53b–17:27

DISCOURSE 18:1–19:1a The Ecclesial Discourse

NARRATIVE 19:1b–23:39

DISCOURSE 24:1–26:1a The Eschatological Discourse

In some instances it is unmistakably clear that the discourse bears on some of the topics and motifs that had appeared in the preceding narrative material. For example, in the stretch of text that runs from 13:53 to 19:1a, the discourse (18:1–19:1) is on the life of the Church. In the narrative section before this, the incidence of ecclesial motifs and themes is noticeably high. Here we have, for example, a series of texts on Simon (Peter): Simon tries to walk on water, as Jesus did (14:28-31); Simon confesses Jesus as Messiah and in turn is named Peter ("the Rock"), for "on this rock I shall build my Church" (16:13-20); Peter is sharply censured for failing to accept the destiny that Jesus reveals as his own (16:21-23); Peter is the haplessly inappropriate speaker at Jesus' transfiguration (17:4-5); he is Jesus' interlocutor when the question of whether Jesus' followers ought to pay the temple tax comes up (17:24-27). Finally, in the discourse on the Church itself, Peter is singled out for special instruction on forgiveness (18:21-22).

Moreover, there are numerous other ecclesial themes in the narrative section preceding the discourse on the Church. For instance, there are two narratives on the feeding of the hungry crowds. Both stories are told with Eucharistic overtones: 14:12b-21, the feeding of the five thousand, consciously alludes to Pentateuchal texts on Israel, the people of God; and 15:32-39, the feeding of the four thousand, is made to allude in equally deliberate fashion to the gentile world and to connote the coming Church of gentiles. Together the two texts intentionally center on the emergence, out of the encounter between Jesus and empirical Israel, of true Israel—that is, of the Church—purified, reshaped, made new.

This, moreover, is precisely the main theme of the first half of chapter 15. The theme culminates in the motif of election put in danger ("Every plant which my heavenly Father has not planted—there is One who shall uproot it," 15:13). Again: there are people-of-God motifs in the transfiguration scene (17:1-8). It is hard to resist the conclusion that the narrative material of chapters 13–17 and the discourse material of chapter 18 are conceived by Matthew as a *thematic unity*. But if this holds for this fourth block of text, it may well hold for the first, second, third, and fifth blocks as well. In fact, this large hypothesis appears to be solidly borne out. So the repeated alternations in *form* (narrative and discourse) signal a set of thematic or *topical* unities, as follows:

Book I: Foundations
— NARRATIVE 3:1–4:25
— DISCOURSE 5:1–7:29
[Sermon on the Mount]

Book II: Jesus' Initiatives
— NARRATIVE 8:1–10:4
— DISCOURSE 10:5–11:1a
[Missionary Discourse]

Book III: Israel's Responses
— NARRATIVE 11:1b–12:50
— DISCOURSE 13:1–53a
[Parables Discourse]

Book IV: The Church
— NARRATIVE 13:53a–17:27
— DISCOURSE 18:1–19:1a
[Ecclesial Discourse]

Book V: The Consummation
— NARRATIVE 19:1b–23:39
— DISCOURSE 24:1–26:1a
[Eschatological Discourse]

b) *Concentric structure*

We should distinguish (a) chiasm/chiasmus, chiasmic/chiastic structure, which has four and only four elements, arranged in the pattern *a-b-b-a*, from (b) "concentric structure," which has three, five, or more elements in the chiasm-like pattern that leads up to and back from a center. Examples: with three elements: *a-b-a*; with five elements: *a-b-c-b-a*; if we add a sixth element: *a-b-c-c-b-a*, the two *c*'s are the center. Or with a seventh element, *d* will be the center, and so on. Are Matthew's five speeches arranged concentrically? If so, the parables discourse is the center.

Moreover, if we look at the parables speech, we will find seven parables:

First parable (4-9)
  Second parable (content: division at the end of time)
    Third parable ⎫
                  ⎬ Paired
    Fourth parable ⎭
    Fifth parable ⎫
                  ⎬ Paired
    Sixth parable ⎭
  Seventh parable
Conclusion (mini-parable)

This is a concentric structure with six elements (if we take the pairing of parables 3 and 4 to constitute one element, and the pairing of parables 5 and 6 to constitute another): *a-b-c / c-b-a*.

Furthermore, between parables 4 and 5 (thus between *c* and *c*) there is a major break: Jesus ceases to address the crowds and begins to speak exclusively to the disciples. At the end of parable 4, Matt 13:34-36 reads as follows: "All this Jesus said to the crowds in parables; indeed he said nothing to them without a parable. This was to fulfill what was spoken by the prophet: 'I will open my mouth in parables, I will utter what has been hidden since the foundation of the world.' Then he left the crowds and went into the house. And his disciples came to him, saying, 'Explain to us . . . ' "

Interpreters have quite rightly seen a shift of some significance right in the middle of the parables speech. The question is whether this shift is of great significance, touching the whole Gospel, or of lesser significance, touching only this chapter. If those who hold the first view are correct, Matt 13:34-36 is the pivot on which the entire Gospel turns. The evangelist is saying: Israel, in full accord with the plan of God, which no one can subvert and defeat, refused the word and act of Jesus; he turned, then, in an act of vast symbolic import, to his disciples . . .

This interpretation is perhaps correct, but it is difficult to settle the matter with full assurance. The shift to the disciples might well be symbolic, but not intended by the evangelist as the pivot of the whole Gospel. So, while it is true that concentric structure is a favorite device of the evangelist, it may be, but is not necessarily, among the principles structuring the whole Gospel.

c) *Geographical structure*

Another way of organizing most of the materials of the Gospel is through a simplified series of settings. For Matthew, where the story is set is more important than when it takes place. He solemnly specifies Galilee as the locale for the beginning of Jesus' proclamation of the Reign of God (Matt 4:12-17). This act of Jesus, writes Matthew, fulfills the prophecy of a great light shining on a people that had lived in darkness and death (4:16).

At what point does Jesus leave Galilee? Probably no earlier than chapter 15. Though "the lonely place" of 14:15 may have originally been understood as outside Galilee (see 14:22), no non-Palestinian place-name appears in the text. The Galilean ministry extends more probably to 15:20. In 15:21 Jesus withdraws to the district of Tyre and Sidon, i.e., as far north, or nearly as far north, as these cities, but inland, where Jews lived among gentiles. Thereafter Jesus is represented as being on the move until the opening of the Jerusalem ministry (Matt 21:1-28:15). The very last scene of the Gospel (Matt 28:16-20) is set, significantly, in Galilee. So from 4:11 to the end of the Gospel, the geographical organization runs as follows:

4:12-15:20	Galilee	21:1-28:15	Jerusalem
15:21-20:34	Journeys	28:16-20	Galilee

d) *Dramatic-and-theological structure*

A datum of maximum significance to the organization of Matthew's Gospel is the role of the Caesarea Philippi pericope (16:13-20) as introducing a whole new phase in Jesus' career. This does not mark the end of anything, for Jesus continues his ministry of proclaiming, teaching, and curing. But this point does mark a new beginning: the beginning of Jesus' effort to prepare his followers *for refusal.* They must not be blown away by refusal. They must not be allowed to lose their confidence in him and his mission and abandon him. They must not be allowed to fall victim to the impending *Ordeal.

How are Jesus' followers to be prepared for the Ordeal and protected from apostasy under its pressure? Jesus seems to provide an answer by projecting some new horizons for their benefit. For the first time he invites his closest followers to say *who he is.* This is just the kind of question that people found themselves drawn to entertain about John the Baptist and about Jesus. *"But who do you* [plural] *say that I am?"* Simon responds: "You are the Messiah, the Son of the living God!" In what follows, Jesus confirms the truth of Simon's confession; assigns a new name to Simon: Peter (Greek: *Petros;* Aramaic: *Kêphā'*), i.e., "Rock"; explains the sense of "rock"; prohibits the disciples from speaking of these things in the open; and, finally, reveals the bitter truth that the nation—in its leadership, the Sanhedrin—runs the risk of turning aside from its own appointed destiny *by refusing the Messiah.* Jesus is indeed on his way to messianic enthronement, but it will be by the path of refusal, suffering, and death. Simon bitterly protests. Jesus just as sharply stifles the protest. These transactions launch the process of preparing the disciples for the future.

If we speak of the opening of a new phase in the drama, we are necessarily talking about some kind of dramatic progression. But what is dramatically progressing? The answer cannot be simply "the career of Jesus," for although Matthew is in some sense offering us a biography of Jesus, he is offering much more than a biography. The presentation of Jesus' career is in the service of ulterior purposes, religious and theological. In Matthew's view, what is dramatically progressing in and through the story of Jesus is an economy of divine revelation and salvation. Concretely, it consists in the *eschatological restoration of Israel. The Caesarea Philippi pericopes open a new phase in this drama of restoration. It will be stamped, delimited, defined by Jesus' death and glorification.

Having isolated this one movement in the progression of the drama, we are inevitably led to ask what other movements or phases are present in the story. The answer turns on two texts, both of them having a solemn, programmatic character like that of the scene at Caesarea Philippi. The first is the editor's introduction to the Galilean ministry (4:12-17), and the second is the "speech of mandate" at the very end of the Gospel (28:16-20).

What this says is, first, that Matthew (and in this he is like Mark) has grasped and presented the material from 3:1-4:11 as "initiation events" prerequisite to Jesus' accomplishment of the divine purpose, the eschatological or definitive restoration of Israel. Second, this work of Jesus, epitomized in the image of the building of the new temple (Matt 16:18—actually, Jesus does not use the temple image but what the image stands for, namely, the assembly or congregation of messianic Israel, his *ekklēsia*), is accomplished in phases. Jesus inaugurates a new phase by preparing his disciples for the dark future that now looms. Finally, the restoration of Israel is to flower in a future hard to imagine: the world mission and the salvation of the gentiles (28:16-20).

These observations lead us to see Matthew's Gospel as organized from 3:1 to 28:20 as follows:

3:1-4:11	Initiation Events
4:12-16:12	Beginning of the Restoration of Israel
16:13-28:15	Consummation of the Restoration of Israel
28:16-20	The Mission of True Israel

Outline of the Gospel of Matthew in Terms of Literary Structure

INFANCY GOSPEL   1:1–2:33

THE MINISTRY OF JESUS   3:1–26:1a

> I. BOOK ONE   3:1–7:29   *Foundations*
>   Narrative   3:1–4:25
>   *Initiation Events*   3:1–4:11
>   *Beginning of the Restoration of Israel*   4:12–16:12
>   *GALILEE*   4:12–15:20
>   Sermon on the Mount   5:1–7:29

> II. BOOK TWO   8:1–11:1a   *Jesus' Initiatives*
>   Narrative   8:1–10:4
>   Missionary Discourse   10:5–11:1a

> III. BOOK THREE   11:1b–13:53a   *Israel's Responses*
>   Narrative   11:1b–12:50
>   Parables Discourse   13:1-53a
>   [*Pivot:* 13:36 Jesus "leaves crowds," turns to disciples]

> IV. BOOK FOUR   13:53b–19:1a   *The Church*
>   Narrative   13:53b–17:27
>   *JOURNEYS*   15:21–20:34
>   *Consummation of the Restoration of Israel*   16:13–28:15
>   Church Discourse   18:1–19:1a

> V. BOOK FIVE   19:1b–26:1a   *The Consummation*
>   Narrative   19:1b–23:39
>   *JERUSALEM*   21:1–28:15
>   Eschatological Discourse   24:1–26:1a

PASSION AND RESURRECTION   26:1b–28:15

> Prologue to the Passion   26:1-46
> The Passion   26:47–27:56
> Interlude   27:57-66
> Empty Tomb   28:1-8
> Appearance to the Women   28:9-10
> Bribing of the Soldiers   28:11-15

> *The Mission of True Israel*   28:16-20

With this analytic outline we leave the complex and rewarding topic of "structure" in Matthew and add a few words about Matthew's style. We have touched on one aspect of that style already: the use of chiastic and concentric arrangements. Some examples doubtless go back directly to the historical Jesus, e.g., 19:30:

> But many that are *first* will be *last*, and the *last first*.

In 20:16 we have the same in reverse order:

> So the *last* will be *first*, and the *first last*.

Matthean style comes to the fore in 12:22 (note: blind-dumb-spoke-saw):

> Then a blind and dumb demoniac was brought to him and he healed him so that the dumb man spoke and saw.

We probably have a Matthean concentric arrangement of words in 13:15 (heart-ears-eyes-eyes-ears-heart):

> For the heart of this people has grown crass
>   and their ears are hard of hearing
>   and their eyes they have closed,
>   lest they should perceive with their eyes
>   and hear with their ears
> and understand with their heart.

A particularly intriguing stylistic development occurs in chapter 23.

I. Woe to you, blind guides, who say,
   "If anyone swears by the sanctuary it is nothing;
   but if anyone swears by the gold of the sanctuary,
      he is bound by his oath."
You blind fools!
Which is greater, the gold or the sanctuary that has made the
      gold sacred?

II. And you say,
   "If anyone swears by the altar it is nothing;

> but if anyone swears by the gift that is on the altar,
>> he is bound by his oath."
>
> You blind men!
> Which is greater, the gift or the altar that makes the gift sacred?
>
> III. So he who swears by the altar
>> swears by it and everything on it,
>
> and he who swears by the sanctuary
>> swears by it and by him who dwells in it,
>
> and he who swears by heaven,
>> swears by the throne of God and by him who sits on it.

Note that in number I the chiasmus is sanctuary-gold-gold-sanctuary; in II it is altar-gift-gift-altar; but III is related to I and II as the second half of a chiasmus: sanctuary (I)-altar (II)-altar-sanctuary (III).

A text that is stylistically as well as thematically rich is the word by which the Matthean Jesus responds to Simon's confession of messianic faith:

> Blessed are you, Simon Bar-Jona,
>> for flesh and blood did not reveal [this] to you,
>> but my heavenly Father!
>
> And I say to you: You are Peter [Rock]
>> and on this rock I will build my Church
>> and the gates of Hades shall not prevail against it.
>
> I will give you the keys to the Reign of heaven
>> and whatever you bind on earth heaven shall bind
>> and whatever you loose on earth heaven shall loose.

This text is among the most perfectly composed in the Gospel. Its background was the bestowal of the name *Petros*/Peter ("Rock") on Simon, probably on the occasion of his confession of Jesus as Messiah. Compare the Johannine text (1:41-42): Andrew cries, " 'We have found the Messiah!' . . . He brought Simon to Jesus, who looked at him and said, 'You are Simon, son of John; you shall be called Cephas' (that is, Peter, 'the Rock')." The texts make clear that the new name given to Simon was, in Aramaic, *Kêphā'*, "(the) Rock." This was translated into Greek, in which the word for "rock, massive rock, bedrock" is *petra*; to function as a man's name, it was given the masculine ending *-os* (*Petros*), despite the fact that the word *petros* in Greek has a sense ("broken rock, pebble") irrelevant to the intended meaning. The name *Kêphā'* is without contemporary parallel; it is attested in the papyri of Elephantine (fifth century B.C.), the postexilic Jewish colony on the island of Elephantine in the Nile.[2] The only meaning that can with real probability be attributed to the name given to Simon by Jesus is the meaning presented by the present text: rock on which to build.

Build what? The Matthean text draws on a specific symbolic scheme—the cosmic rock—which alone explains the imagery of the whole text. The cosmic rock is the foundation of the world-sanctuary; it is the lid over the underworld (cf. "gates of Hades"); and the sanctuary marks the point of access to the abode of God, the gates of heaven (cf. "keys to the Reign of heaven"). In Jesus' adaptation of the cosmic-rock imagery, "my (messianic) congregation/assembly" takes the place of the image of the sanctuary or temple. Just as Yahweh said of Eliakim, son of Hilkiah, "I shall place the key of David's palace on his shoulder; what he opens none will shut, and what he shuts none will open" (Isa 22:22), so Jesus entrusts Simon-the-Rock with "the keys to the Reign of heaven" and the plenipotentiary status of householder in the economy of salvation.

The stylistic traits of the text accent its indissolubility as a triad; the three verses constitute a single unit. Each unit has three lines: the first line, a thematic statement, is followed by an explanatory couplet cast in antithetical parallelism (second and third lines). So "Blessed are you" is explained by: *not* flesh and blood *but* heavenly Father (revealed this). "You are the Rock" is explained by: *atop* the rock, I build my Church; *below* the rock, gates of Hades rage in vain. "Keys to the Reign of heaven" is explained by: *binding* will truly bind, *loosing* will truly loose.

The original language of these words was in all probability Aramaic; in parts of the text the idiom is not that of Jesus but that of the Matthean tradition (*"heavenly* Father," "Reign *of heaven"*). The text exhibits a high artistry; whether redactional or pre-redactional it is difficult to say.

These examples of artistry in structure and style are meant to alert us in advance to the compositional procedures we shall find in the speeches.

The Theology of Matthew

What kind of theology is at work in the storytelling that is Matthew's Gospel? Quite clearly it is neither the rhetorical theology that came into being in the patristic period (second to eighth century) nor the systematic theology that came into being in the Middle Ages. For want of a better name, it is "biblical theology," and to be more specific, it is kerygmatic theology. It derives from the central message or kerygma of Jesus. Hence its key terms are: the Reign of God (it has in one sense already arrived!); the restoration of Israel (it is a definitive economy of salvation already in operation!); the final revelation of God, for Jesus has revealed God as Father. Moreover, the revelation of Jesus is a self-revelation: he is the Christ, the Son of the living God, the Son of Man, and Servant of the Lord; his task is the salvation of Israel and the nations.

This shows how far removed Matthew's theology is from a structure worked out in the "intellectual pattern" of experience. Matthean theology derives rather from a lived, holistic experience of salvation. "Experience": there is first the pre-Easter life of the disciples. The author of canonical Matthew, to be sure, is not one of these disciples but rather an early heir. If the lived experience of salvation is also the Easter experience of the disciples, he shares this experience, once again not in person but only as an early heir of the truth of the resurrection. The point at which Matthew speaks from firsthand experience is as a churchman of the first century who has witnessed the break between the Church and the Synagogue. Inheriting this break and responding to it, Matthew's Gospel deals harshly with the Jewish religious elite of competitors and enemies of Christ.

Again, a point at which Matthew speaks from firsthand experience is the launching of the world mission. It had been fully launched with the pivotal decision of the Church at the so-called Council of Jerusalem (probably in the late forties). Matthew's Gospel was written a single generation later, when the mission was in full force. Part of his contribution to the religious grasp of this commanding facet of the life of the first-century Church lay in rooting it in the story of Jesus, specifically in his resurrection. Matthew's text, moreover, is designed not only to make the mission intelligible but to serve as a missionary instrument of instruction. Matthew presents the risen Christ mandating the teaching of "all that I have enjoined on you" (Matt 28:20). His Gospel is a handbook allowing the missionaries to do just that.

What kind of response from the readers of the Gospel does Matthew seek to elicit? There can be no doubt that his audience was as wide as the mission field, including the mixed Church of Jews and gentiles in Antioch, as well as Jews and gentiles in the mission field of the Mediterranean basin. Despite this great diversity, we can answer the question in general terms. He seeks, above all, a religious response. But he is writing a story, not a tract. What he presents as appealing for a response is not an idea but a drama. It is not a fictional but a historical drama. Above all, its chief figure is not fictional. He is a living being. The selfsame figure who was born in Bethlehem, lived in Galilee, and died outside the city wall of Jerusalem is now risen, enthroned, and glorified. By his recounting of the story of Jesus, Matthew aims at creating the conditions for an encounter with Christ.

Matthew is a creative editor. He has inherited almost all his materials. His task is to shape them into a new whole that will mediate a personal encounter with Jesus. Out of this encounter, Matthew hopes, faith in Jesus as the saving messianic Lord and Son of God will arise. His editorial task is, therefore, most demanding. He has met it partly by simplifying (for example, his account of Jesus' miracles sacrifices colorful elements found in Mark's Gospel, such as drama, setting, graphic but distracting detail, to the sober requisites of the theologically conscious catechist), partly by unveiling the full complexity of Jesus' historic task. The complexity of his task calls for more than a collection of anecdotes, no matter how charged with meaning. In view of the response he aims at eliciting from his readers, Matthew finds himself obliged to ground the intended response in a full, grandiose, and total vision of Christ and his mission.

One of Matthew's ways of achieving this is by taking discrete materials, correlating them thematically, and giving them the finished structure of speeches. He probably had a model in the Sermon on the Mount, for, as we shall see in the next chapter, a brilliant piece of literary criticism has shown that Matthew found in his source material a sermon that he further developed. The result is a Matthean masterpiece.

We should make it clear that the object of the present modest study is the intended meaning of the five great speeches in the Gospel of Matthew. These speeches put us in contact with the real Jesus of ancient Palestine. Still, they are also the positive accomplishment of Matthew, a great religious artist and the best of the catechetical theologians of the New Testament. How well he has served the Church of all times we shall see in the course of the following chapters on five still powerful speeches that are still changing the world.

Chapter 2

THE SERMON ON THE MOUNT

(Matthew 5:1–7:29)

We may begin with homage to Jacques Dupont for his remarkably successful and useful study, a generation ago, of the Sermon on the Mount in Matthew and the Sermon on the Plain in Luke.[3] What Dupont shows is how profitable a close verse-by-verse study of parallels between the two speeches might be. First of all, it becomes clear that they are two versions of what was originally one speech; second, it becomes equally clear in the light of verse-by-verse analysis that the Matthean speech cannot be explained as a rewriting of the Lukan speech; nor is it at all plausible that Luke's speech is a straightforward rewriting of Matthew's. Both inherited a single speech, and each dealt with it in eminently understandable and typical fashion. Matthew enlarged the speech, drawing on materials from elsewhere in the tradition to illustrate, emphasize, and fill out. Luke shortened the speech, dropping materials less immediately understandable and relevant to gentiles than to Jews, and highlighting materials of keener interest to pagan converts.

From the start there is a solid and unambiguous observation: Where material was common to Matthew's and Luke's sermon, it appeared in the same order. Of great interest, then, was the answer to the question of where each item that was unparalleled in either speech came from. If a given piece of material appeared in Luke only, the question was: Did Mat-

thew omit it from the sermon, or did Luke add it from elsewhere in the fund of tradition (or produce it himself)? If
material appeared in Matthew only, the questions were the reverse: Did Luke omit it from the sermon as it stood in the
source, or did Matthew add it to the sermon from elsewhere
in the tradition?

Patterns turned up. Matthew's sermon was much longer
than Luke's, and this, no doubt, for two reasons. There were
many instances in which the question about material that appeared only in Matthew called for the answer: Matthew added
it from elsewhere in the tradition. An example is the Our Father. Its location in Matthew's Gospel is in the Sermon on the
Mount; in Luke's Gospel it is in the travel narrative that runs
from chapter 9 to chapter 18. Though it is possible to imagine
one or another motive for Luke's dropping it from the sermon,
no really precise or persuasive reason comes to mind. Nothing, on the other hand, is easier than to say why Matthew
might have introduced the prayer here from elsewhere in the
tradition. He had found in his source for the sermon a general
principle (avoid practicing your righteousness in public) and
three applications (avoid publicizing your almsgiving; avoid
making a pious spectacle of public prayer; avoid fasting in conspicuous fashion).

Apropos of the second application, regarding prayer, Matthew's final version of the sermon offers a text on avoiding
long prayers with many words: "Do not babble away as the
gentiles do, for they imagine their prayers will be answered
if only they use words enough!" Notice that though this text
is on prayer, it is not really to the point, namely, avoiding con-
spicuously *public* prayer. All the more reason to think that Matthew himself introduced this motif regarding long prayers into
the sermon on the general principle that Jesus' inaugural
speech should be comprehensive. Matthew reasoned, in other
words: If the topic of prayer comes up, Jesus must be made
to give his main teachings on prayer. This surely must include
the Our Father. *Conclusion:* Luke did not omit the Our Father
from the common source; rather, Matthew added it here from

elsewhere in the tradition to fill out concretely the general category of prayer.

The first result of applying this kind of analysis to the materials of the sermon is that we discover why Matthew's sermon is longer than Luke's. A second result is that we gradually uncover the contours of the sermon as it stood in the source common to Matthew and Luke. This is the form it had:

Exordium: Four Beatitudes (Matt 5:3, 4, 6, 11)

Part One: Perfect Righteousness
  Lead theme (Matt 5:17, 20)
  Five instances (5:21-24, 27-28, 33-37, 38-42, 43-48)

Part Two: Good Works
  Lead theme (6:1)
  Three instances (6:2-4, 5-6, 16-18)

Part Three: Warnings
  Do not condemn (7:1-2); the speck and the log (7:3-5)
  False prophets (7:15); the tree and the fruits (7:16-20)
  Hear and act! (7:21); house on rock and house on sand
  (7:24-27)

What did Matthew do with this legacy of tradition? Primarily, he kept it as it was; secondarily, he added, enriched, filled out. The materials used to fill out came from elsewhere in the tradition of Jesus' words. (Lukan parallels to the Matthean additions are found mostly in the Lukan travel narrative.) And the point of Matthew's additions? No doubt it was to underscore the programmatic character of the sermon—a purpose brilliantly achieved. But there was a price to pay: This obscured the clean lines of the sermon as it existed in the pre-Matthean source. In the end we find ourselves compelled to admit that the sermon in its final Matthean form is overloaded both structurally and thematically. For example, the simple exordium in the source (four beatitudes) becomes, in Matthew, a threefold introduction:

Again, in Matt 6:19-34 the material on "cares" coheres only loosely with the rest of the sermon. On the other hand, who would readily give up the beatitudes as we find them in Matthew? And if the introduction to the sermon is overloaded, we might be tempted to say, "So much the better!" Moreover, the section on "cares" is a gem. It is all the more charged with meaning from the bare fact that Matthew has highlighted it as fully deserving inclusion in Jesus' first great speech. The theme gains power from the sheer fact of belonging to a speech that has ranked—from its first hearers, through the liturgy of the ages, to such modern students as Mohandas Gandhi and Martin Luther King—as the greatest speech of all time.

To complete the outline of Matthew's Sermon on the Mount, we should add to the introductions listed above the following four constituent parts:

We shall follow this outline in dealing with the substance of the sermon.

INTRODUCTION, Phase One: NINE BEATITUDES

5:3 **Happy the poor in spirit, for theirs is the Reign of heaven!**

4 **Happy those in mourning, for there is One who shall comfort them!**

5 **Happy the humble, for they shall inherit the land!**

6 **Happy those who hunger and thirst for righteousness, for there is One who shall give them their fill!**

7 **Happy the merciful, for there is One who shall show them mercy!**

8 **Happy the single-hearted, for they shall see God!**

9 **Happy the peacemakers, for God shall make them his sons!**

10 **Happy those persecuted for their quest of righteousness, for theirs is the Reign of heaven!**

11 **Happy are you when people berate you and persecute you and lie about you because of me!**

12 **Be cheered and be glad; your reward from God will be great, for this is how they persecuted the prophets before you.**

5:3: The standard translation is "Blessed," but "Happy" is just as accurate. Likewise, the name "macarism" is as accurate as "beatitude."

"Poor in spirit": This conversion of a social category into a religious one mirrors an earlier evolution in biblical tradition from before the Babylonian Exile (587–537 B.C.), when those literally poor were the object of prophetic protection, to the Exile and afterward, when "the poor" became a term for those who, having nothing, learn to lean on God, and whom God especially cherishes and protects. The Matthean beatitude has changed "poor" to "poor in spirit": those who feel spiritual, or religious, need. (In the Pharisaic Psalms of Solomon, the Pharisees refer to themselves as "the poor"; but Matthew's "poor in spirit" are the very opposite of the Pharisees as Matthew portrays them.)

5:4, 6, 7, 9: The translations are meant to reflect the use of *"the divine passive."

5:8: "Single-hearted": literally "pure (or) clean of heart." The pure heart is "unalloyed, undivided, simple, single."

5:9: "They shall be called" is the same as "they shall become"; the translation takes account of the use here of the divine passive.

5:12: According to Judaic tradition, suffering and martyrdom belong to the prophetic vocation.

Main Thrust

In the Bible there are two kinds of beatitude: the apocalyptic kind, which promises the blessings of eschatological salvation to variously designated beneficiaries, and the sapiential kind, which enunciates the principle of blessings on the virtuous. Jesus' original beatitudes were apocalyptic; the tendency of Matthean editing is to convert them to the sapiential kind.

The first (and oldest) beatitudes are paradoxes: Happy the *poor*? Those *in mourning*? The *humble*? Yes! Why? *Because God was about to reverse their situation!* In place of this original accent Matthew has introduced a new idea: All those are "happy" who are destined for divine reward. But reward is for virtue. Therefore, the poor must become "the poor in spirit." It similarly makes sense to suppose that some virtue is being attributed to "those in mourning." What is it? The sobriety of those who acknowledge the present life as a vale of tears? Again, the original sense of "the humble" was those who had nothing (the biblical "poor, afflicted, lowly"). Now it comes to mean those who are unpretentious and self-effacing. The hungry to whom God was on the point of giving their fill now become those who hunger and thirst *for righteousness*; they shall be filled—with the righteousness they have longed for.

But it is perhaps not fair to contrast Matthew's beatitudes with those of Jesus. We will do well to consider the Matthean form without prejudice, for its own sake. Greek philosophers, e.g., Aristotle, managed to penetrate to a great truth: The happy life is the good life. Matthew offers a religious hold on a comparable truth: They are truly happy who are happy in the long run and in the last resort. These are those whom God accepts and rewards in the judgment and the life to come. It is worth remarking that the merciful are humble practitioners of an aristocratic virtue;[4] the single-hearted are the pure of heart, who will one thing: the will of God; the peacemakers are, again, ordinary folk who have had another aristocratic or royal virtue brought within their ken and within reach of ordinary daily life. Finally, those persecuted for their quest of righteousness and those persecuted for belonging to the party of the rejected Messiah, Jesus, are promised reversal and reward.

Their reward is scheduled for the coming of the messianic judge: the Reign of God. This is the comfort of God, who "will wipe every tear from their eyes" (Rev 21:4); the land of promise, not Canaan/Palestine but what this land symbolized: salvation, or the whole world made new at the end of time (see Rom 4:13); the mercy of the divine judge; the vision of God; sonship to God in its full, final dimension of ease, intimacy, joy, and love.

INTRODUCTION, Phase Two: METAPHORS OF SALT AND LIGHT

5:13   **You are the salt of the earth!**
        But if salt becomes insipid, how will its tang be restored?
        It is good for nothing but to be thrown out and trampled underfoot!

14   **You are the light of the world!**
        No city set on a mountain can be hidden.

15   **Nor do people light a lamp only to put it under a bushel-basket.**
        No, they put it on a lampstand
        and it gives light to all in the house.

16   **Let your light so shine before men**
        that, seeing your good actions,
        they give praise to your heavenly Father.

5:13-16: The addressees especially envisaged are the disciples of Jesus. The Church is implicitly invited to identify with them and to hear Jesus' voice and words as addressed to themselves.

5:14-15: In rabbinic literature (e.g., *Rabba* to Canticle of Canticles 1, 3), "Israel is the light of the world." Again, in a rabbinic text (*Sifre*, Numbers) Moses is compared to "a lamp placed on a lampstand."

Main Thrust

This second phase of the introduction is an appeal to the audience to live up to its vocation. In the idiom of the poet Pindar, this is to "become what thou art." In the language of the Apostle Paul, it is to be "transformed by the newness of your spirit" (Rom 12:2). How are the hearers to live up to their calling as "the salt of the earth" and "the light of the world"? This is just the question that this introductory passage is designed to evoke. The answer will be given by the speech as a whole.

INTRODUCTION, Phase Three: JESUS AND THE LAW

5:17   **Do not think that I have come**
      to take away from the Law or the prophets.
    I have come not to take away,
      but to bring to completion!
18   **For, amen I say to you:**
    Before heaven and earth pass away,
    not a letter, not a pen-stroke, will pass from the Law;
    rather, everything must come to fulfillment.
19   **If anyone then suppresses even the least of the Law's precepts**
    and teaches others to do the same,
    God will make him the least in the Reign of heaven.
    But whoever observes them and teaches others to do the same
    God will make the greatest in the Reign of heaven.

5:17:   What does the word *plērōsai* ("fulfill") mean? Our main clue is the contrast between the words "destroy" or "annul" and "fulfill." This contrast suggests that we interpret the second verb, as Jacques Dupont puts it, "in the sense of: 'to bring to its completion, to its full measure, to its perfection.'"

5:18:   "Rather, everything must come to fulfillment": this "everything" is not limited to the Law but includes Law, promise, prophecy, foreshadowing, aspiration, secrets to be revealed.

20 I tell you:
    **Unless your righteousness is better than that of the scribes
    and the Pharisees,
    you will not enter the Reign of heaven at all.**

Main Thrust

This climactic part of the introduction will lead directly into
the antitheses between the teaching of the scribes past and
present and the teaching of Jesus on the Law. Jesus was ac-
cused of detracting from the Law. He here proclaims that his
God-given task is by no means to subtract, but to bring the
Law to that fullness and completion that had been divinely appointed for the end of time. For the first time we are introduced
to the theme of "eschatological measure." The idea is that God
has appointed a certain crowning completion of his revelation
to Israel; Jesus calls on his hearers to interpret him in just these
terms. If he differs from the elite of Israel's teachers (scribes
or sages) on Sabbath observance, on dealing and dining with
notorious sinners, on oaths, on reverence for the temple, this
is not a sign that he is chipping away at the Torah. Just the
opposite—it is a sign that he is bringing the Torah to the completion intended by God, a completion reserved for the climactic and definitive (messianic!) revelation to his people.

Christian teachers must follow this tack, not accommodat-
ing to the world and suppressing selected parts of the Law,
but affirming it in its entirety and teaching the Church to do
the same.

This is primarily meant to reject the false liberalism of many
Pharisees, but perhaps there is a secondary undertone in the
text. A perfect example of the ideal presented here was James,
"the brother (i.e., relative) of the Lord," who, according to

---

5:20: "Righteousness" is what makes the human subject pleasing to God. Judaism took this to be "observance of the Law"; Matthew presents it as the full response to the Messiah's bringing of the
Law to its foreordained measure of completeness.

the early Christian writer Hegesippus, accommodated to the Law in every particular that accorded with Christian faith. The admonition to Christian teachers may, then, be meant to say: Be like James (not Paul)! If this is an accurate reading, we would have here an indication of how early traditions were read in, say, the fifties of the first century.

MAIN BODY: PART ONE, THE ANTITHESES

5:21 You have heard that the men of old were told:
    "Thou shalt not murder; the murderer deserves condemnation (to death)."

22 But I say to you:
    Whoever gets angry at his brother merits condemnation (to death).
    Whoever says to his brother, "You blockhead!" merits the [(death-) sentence of the] high court;
    Whoever says "You idiot!" merits condemnation to the fiery pit.

23 If, then, while having your (expiatory) offering brought to the altar (of holocausts) you (suddenly) remember that your brother (still) has a grievance against you, (postpone the

24 sacrifice and) • leave your offering before the altar, and (first) go and bring about reconciliation between yourself and your brother, and then come back and have your sacrifice offered.

25 Come to terms with the plaintiff who sues you, quickly, while you are with him on the way (to court), or he may hand you over to (condemnation by) the judge and the judge hand you over to the guard and you be thrown into prison.

26 Amen, I tell you, once in you will not get out till you pay the last penny.

5:21-22: The translation reflects the detailed philological work of Gustaf Dalman and Joachim Jeremias.

5:25-26: This is the imagery of non-Jewish legal practice, which Jesus often used in his parables.

27 You have heard that it was said:
"Thou shalt not commit adultery."
28 But I say to you:
Whoever looks at a woman lustfully
has already committed adultery with her in his heart.
29 But if one of your eyes makes you fall,
tear it out and throw it away,
for it is better to lose a part of your body
than to have God throw the whole of it into the pit.
30 And if one of your hands makes you fall,
cut it off and throw it away,
for it is better to lose one of your limbs
than to have your whole body go into the pit.
31 Our forefathers were told:
"Whoever divorces his wife must give her a certificate of
divorce."
32 But I say to you:
Whoever divorces his wife
(except in the case of [Levitical] incest)
makes her commit adultery
and whoever marries a divorced woman commits adultery
with her.

5:27-28: It is characteristic of the high, eschatological idealism of the sermon that in strictly moral terms an internal act such as lust should be interpreted as on a par with an external act such as adultery. (Obviously, the moral code that Jesus presents is as far removed as possible from "pragmatic" norms, from "feel good" morality, and the like.)

5:29-30: The statements, powerful figures of speech, are meant metaphorically; that they are not meant literally by no means signifies that they are not meant seriously.

5:31-32: "(Except in the case of [Levitical] incest)" seems to be, so far, the best interpretation of Matthew's "exceptive clause." ("Except on the ground of adultery" is not probable; Matthew, like the other evangelists, understands the prohibition of divorce-remarriage in the most rigorous sense.) What seems to be forbidden is non-observance of Levitical prohibitions of "incest." (This may well be the explanation of what the decree of James in Acts 15:19-20 prohibits among gentile Christians who live in mixed Church communities with Jewish Christians.)

33 Again, you have heard that the men of old were told:
     "Thou shalt perform to the Lord what thou hast sworn."
34 But I say to you:
     Do not swear at all!
     Neither "by heaven," for heaven is God's throne,
35   nor "earth," for the earth is his footstool,
     nor "by Jerusalem," for Jerusalem is the city of the great
       king.
36   You must not swear by your head,
     for you cannot turn so much as a single hair white or black.
37   Rather, let your every yes be yes and your every no be no.
     Anything beyond that comes from the evil one.
38 You have heard that it was said:
     "No more than an eye for an eye
     and no more than a tooth for a tooth."
39 But I say to you:
     Do not set yourself at all against the man who wrongs you;
     but if someone slaps you on the right cheek,
       turn the other to him, too;
40   and if someone wants to sue you and take your tunic,
       let him have your cloak as well;
41   and if someone requisitions you for a mile,
       do two miles with him.
42   Give to the beggar
     and do not turn away from the borrower.
43 You have heard that it was said:
     "Thou shalt love thy neighbor, though thine adversary thou
     needst not love."

5:33-35: In Judaism of the century leading up to Jesus' time, the
use of oaths had become commonplace. Jesus' solution is the most
radical on record: Do not use oaths at all! (This was meant to put an
end to spontaneous, intemperate practice; it did not prohibit oaths
that were, so to speak, "officially" required.) Jesus was hypersensi-
tive to all sins of speech, not just to lying.

5:43: The translation adopts the most likely original sense of Jesus'
words (Paul Joüon, Joachim Jeremias), in which "but you shall hate
your enemy = you need not love your personal enemy or adversary"
is a casuistic limitation of the scope of "Thou shalt love thy neighbor
(= fellow countryman; fellow Jew)." Some examples in which "hate"

44 But I say to you:
        Love your enemies and pray for those who persecute you,
45   that you may become children of your heavenly Father,
        who has his sun rise on good and bad alike
        and makes the rain fall on the innocent and the guilty.
46   For if you love only those who love you,
        what recompense do you deserve?
        Do not even publicans do the same?
47   And if you reserve your greetings for your friends,
        what are you doing beyond the required?
        Do not even gentiles do the same?
48   Therefore, "ye shall be perfect"
        as your heavenly Father is perfect.

Main Thrust

This first part of the sermon goes beyond the Law/Torah of Sinai to propose the Law/Torah of Zion, appointed and reserved for the end-time: "For out of Zion shall go forth the Law and the word of the LORD from Jerusalem" (Isa 2:3d). This, as the Gospel of Matthew will gradually make clear, is messianic Law, a code of messianic discipleship. We are far removed from the mountain in the Sinai wilderness; we are dealing with a code deriving from the distinctive self-revelation of the Messiah, Son of the living God. So the better righteousness of Matt 5:20 is not merely the better observance of a Law already long hallowed by tradition; it is a Law now, at this moment, being made new. It does retrieve the Law of Moses, but now it brings that Law to the crowning completion that God had appointed for it.

---

signifies "not-to-love/not-to-prefer": Gen 29:31; Mal 1:2-3. The modal expression "thou needst not" is a reflection of the Aramaic substratum: the Aramaic imperfect tense is less commonly future ("shall") than modal ("may, must," etc.).

5:48: "Ye shall be perfect" would seem a free citation of Deut 18:13. This highest ideal of human fulfillment in the image of God caps both the last antithesis and the whole series.

It is true that Jesus found fault with the Pharisees for the lip service they paid to a Law that they understood but failed to observe (e.g., Matt 23:2-4, 13-14, 23-24). But this was by no means the whole of the Matthean Christ's view of the Pharisees. Like the rest of Israel's religious elite (the priests, the theologians, or "scribes," whether Pharisees or Sadducees), these pious men, the Pharisees, understood themselves to be in firm possession of a self-sufficient system. Anyone who claimed to bring to Israel a new and indispensable completion of divine revelation, as both John and Jesus did, would meet confident and fierce opposition, for the majority of these critics had closed themselves off in advance from the element of the new, the unforeseen, the unexpected. Unlike the prophets of old, they refused to recognize that there were problems inherent in the human situation constituting a chronic threat to salvation (the heart most crooked, beyond remedy—Jer 17:9; a rebellious spirit and a heart of stone—Ezek 36:26-27), which the Law of Moses had left intact. Hence, they repudiated the vital contrary supposition of Jesus, that of radical need on the part of all: "Unless you repent [i.e., accept and act on my message], you will all likewise perish!" (Luke 13:3).

Consider the six antitheses:

You have heard it said:	*but I tell you:*
not to murder . . .	not even to say "Blockhead" or "Idiot"!
not to commit adultery . . .	not even to glance lustfully!
not to divorce without giving a divorce certificate . . .	not to divorce at all!
not to swear an oath without fulfilling it . . .	not to swear an oath at all!
not to take vengeance beyond an eye for an eye . . .	not to take vengeance at all!
to love your neighbor (unless he is an adversary) . . .	to love even your enemies!

Notice that in every instance Jesus has radicalized the Law of Moses, making it more demanding. But once again there was a vital supposition behind this increase in demand: the disciple of Jesus has been transformed. Later in the sermon Jesus will say: Only a good tree bears good fruit (Matt 7:17-18). If the eye is clear, it is because the whole body is full of light (Matt 6:22). The follower of Jesus and of his new Law is a changed person: a good tree, a body full of light, salt of the earth, and light of the world. (Such "transformation" was not a prominent issue during Jesus' public career; it is accordingly not a theme of the Sermon on the Mount. Rather, it is a supposition that runs through the Gospel of Matthew, now and again breaking surface, e.g., as the boundless power of God made available to the disciple *by faith*—Matt 17:20; 19:26.)

MAIN BODY: PART TWO, DO NOT PRACTICE YOUR RIGHTEOUSNESS IN PUBLIC

6:1 **Be on guard against practicing your righteousness in public**
for people to see, for if you do you will have no recompense
from your heavenly Father.

2 **But when you give alms,**
do not have a trumpet blown in front of you,
as the hypocrites do in the synagogues and streets
to make people praise them.
Amen, I say to you:
they have all the recompense they are going to get.

3 **But when you give alms**
your own left hand should not know
what your right hand is doing,

4 **so that your giving may be secret,**
and your Father who sees what is secret will reward you.

5 **And when you pray,**
do not be like the hypocrites,
who like to say their prayers
in the synagogues and on the corners of the squares to let
people see them.
Amen, I say to you:
they have all the recompense they are going to get.

6:2: "Trumpet": a metaphor.

6   But when you pray,
        "enter your room and shut your door"
        and pray to your Father who is unseen
        and your Father who sees the unseen will reward you.
7   When you pray, do not babble away as the gentiles do, for
        they imagine that their prayers will be answered if only they
8   use words enough. • Do not be like them, for your Father
        knows what you need before you ask him.
9   Here, then, is how to pray:
        Our heavenly Father,
        Let your name be hallowed!
10   Let your Reign come!
        Let your good pleasure be done
        on earth as in heaven!

6:6: "Enter your room and shut your door" probably cites Isa 26:20. If this is correct, Jesus' citation may, like the Isaian text itself, imply the divinely wrought crisis situation as the context of the prayer. (Jesus vision of the future, as we shall see especially in the second and the fifth of the five speeches, prominently focused on the looming "time of distress" that would precede the advent of the Reign of God. See *Ordeal.)

6:7: For the same reason, prayer is to be short.

6:9-10: The first two petitions (on "name" and "Reign") derive from Jewish liturgy, namely from the "Holy Prayer, or *Qaddiš*, with which the synagogue service ended and which was doubtless familiar to Jesus from childhood. The oldest form of the prayer:

> Let his great name be glorified and hallowed in the world he created in accord with his good pleasure.
> Let his kingly dominion reign in your lifetime and in your days and in the lifetime of the whole house of Israel, speedily and soon. Amen.

Thanks to the *Qaddiš*, we can be reasonably sure of the sense of the petitions in the Our Father. "Let your name be hallowed!" means "Let the acclamation ring out!" The reference is to the hallowing of God's name in the joyous acclamation, the "new song" (Isa 42:10), that will greet and acknowledge the consummation of God's final saving act. The petition, then, is not the expression of a pious hope that people will be reverent toward the name of God; it is a cry for the eschaton, for the divine triumph that will release a cascade of praise

11   Our bread of tomorrow
       give us today;
12   and cancel our debts
       as we (hereby) cancel those of our debtors.
13   And do not let us fall victim to temptation,
       but deliver us from evil.

"from the end of the earth" (Isa 42:10). "Let your name be hallowed!" is in perfectly synonymous *parallelism with "Let your Reign come!"

6:11: "Our bread of tomorrow": This supposes that the rare Greek adjective *epiousios*, mistakenly translated into Latin by *cotidianus* and into English by "daily," ought to have been translated into Latin by *crastinus* and into English by "of tomorrow." We have a solid confirmation from St. Jerome, who reported that in the targum-like Aramaic version of Matthew, the Gospel of the Nazoreans, the Our Father text on bread had *mahar* ("tomorrow)." There is a good reason for thinking that this is so significant. The translator of Matthew, when he got to this point in the text, surely wrote down the Our Father as he daily prayed it all his life. In other words, the Aramaic text of the Our Father long antedated the retroversion of Matthew's Gospel into Aramaic. It went back, no doubt, to the origins of Christianity.

Now what does this "tomorrow" mean? It most probably refers to the future day of salvation, when, as Jesus promised, we shall banquet with the patriarchs in the Reign of God (Matt 8:11). The prayer says: Give us, even today, an advance taste of this future banquet of salvation, for we desperately need it! (It is not in the least surprising that many Christians in antiquity identified this foretaste of "our bread of tomorrow" with the Eucharist.)

6:12: "Our debts" is an Aramaism for "our sins" or "offenses." "As we (hereby) cancel": The prayer provides the occasion for forgiving others. We learn this from the strange use, in Greek, of the aorist tense (*aphēkamen*); it is best explained as rendering an Aramaic "perfect of coincidence" expressing the simultaneous acts of forgiveness of God and of the reciter of the prayer. Paul Joüon emphasizes that the "action of forgiving is accomplished at the very moment at which the speaker speaks" (*L'Évangile*, 35). In short, the phrase "we (hereby) cancel" is a performative speech act: with these words we place the act of cancelling.

6:13: "And do not let us fall victim to temptation": In the original version, taught by the historical Jesus, "temptation" doubtless referred to the Ordeal, or great tribulation, which was conceived as imminent. To Matthew, however, the tribulation is postponed to an

14   For, if you forgive people their offenses,
      your heavenly Father will forgive you too.

15   But if you do not forgive people their offenses,
      neither will your heavenly Father forgive you yours.

16 When you fast,
      do not look gloomy like the hypocrites,
      for they neglect their appearance
      to let people know that they are fasting.
    Amen, I say to you:
      they have all the recompense they are going to get.

17 But when you fast,
      anoint your head and wash your face

18   so that no one can see that you are fasting
      except your Father who is unseen
      and your Father who sees the unseen will reward you.

Main Thrust

For the modern Christian, who might tend to shrug off the notion of recompense, the force of the text might be conveyed thus: For if you make your pious practices public, they will be utterly valueless, they will count for nothing, before your heavenly Father! According to the religious and theological conceptions that Jesus shared with Palestinian Judaism generally, "recompense" is not an optional extra; it is concretely fused with the moral and religious worth of good action. Recompense and value are not to be thought of as one and the same, but they were inseparable.

This is merely meant to sharpen our eye for the main thrust of this part of the sermon: to devalue the social prestige of piety. Jesus says: "Recompense, yes, but from your heavenly

---

indefinite future (as we shall see in the last great speech in Matthew's Gospel). The difference of meaning is real, but the two meanings are related. In both the petitioners beg: Save us from ourselves! Above all, do not let us become apostates under pressure! ("Lead us not" mistranslates "Do not allow us to go." The rest of the text would read literally "into the (power of)." But "to go into the power of" is "to fall victim to."

Father. Do not look for recompense from a human public!"
There is a subtlety and discernment in Jesus' view of good
deeds. You should carefully avoid falling into the trap of prestige piety, but this will not prevent you from being the city
on the mountain. It will not stop you from bringing light to
the world. Act in accord with the will of your heavenly Father,
hiding your piety—praying and giving alms and fasting in
secret—and your light will still shine, not to your own glory
but to the glory of your heavenly Father.

MAIN BODY: PART THREE, LIVE FREE OF "CARES"

6:19 Do not accumulate treasures on earth
      where moth and rust consume
      and where thieves bore through and steal.

20 But accumulate treasures in heaven
      where neither moth nor rust consumes
      nor thieves bore through and steal.

21 For wherever your treasure is,
      there will your heart be too.

22 The eye is the lamp of the body:
      if your eye is healthy, (it is a sign that)
      your whole body is full of light;

23   but if your eye is unhealthy, (it is a sign that)
      your whole body is dark.
      But if your very light is darkness,
      how deep will the darkness be!

24 No slave can belong to two masters,
      for he will prefer one to the other
      or stand by one and disdain the other.
      You cannot serve God and Mammon!

25 Therefore, I say to you:
      Do not be anxious, for your soul's sake, about having some-
      thing to eat,

6:22-23: The clear eye is a metaphor for good judgment, the bad
eye for bad judgment. The judgment in question is the value judgment that leads to faith.
   6:25: "For your soul's sake": the conception operative in the He-

      nor, for your body's sake, about having something to wear.
      Is not the soul more than food
      and the body more than clothing?

26 Look at how the wild birds
      neither sow nor reap nor gather into barns,
      and yet your heavenly Father feeds them.
      Are you not more important than they?

27   But which of you for all his worrying
      could add so much as an hour to his life?

28 And why should you worry about clothing?
      Look at how the wild lilies grow!
      They do not toil or spin,

29   yet I tell you, not even Solomon in all his glory
      was arrayed like one of them.

30   But if God so clothes the wild grass
      that is alive today and thrown into the furnace tomorrow,
      will he not much more surely clothe you,
        O men of little faith?

31   So do not worry, asking,
      "What shall we have to eat?"
      or "What shall we have to wear?"

32   for these are all things the gentiles pursue,
      and your heavenly Father knows that you need them all.

33 But seek first his Reign and righteousness,
      and there is One who will give you all these things as well.

34 So do not worry about tomorrow; let tomorrow worry about
      itself.
      "Sufficient unto the day is the evil thereof."

---

brew Bible is that the soul is the seat of hunger. (This does not necessarily imply a view of the human subject as a body-soul composite.) "Is not the soul more than food?" is not meant to invite an affirmation of the worth of the soul. It is meant rather to say: "Not on bread alone doth man live." One might translate loosely, "Is not life more than food?"

6:25-33: This text, often misinterpreted under the mistaken impression that Jesus makes the birds and flowers models of indifference to the practicalities of life, proposes the way of God and his benevolence as the ground of trust and confidence. It is an *a fortiori* argument: If God so cares for the birds and flowers, how much more will he care for you?

6:34c: Probably a popular proverb.

Main Thrust

The theme of "cares" raises the question: Exactly what is it that Jesus commends? Has he come out here against "prudence" and "planning," on grounds that it is completely futile ("which of you for all his worrying could add so much as an hour to his life?"), and in favor of a hand-to-mouth and day-by-day existence? In what sense do the wild birds and lilies give us a clue as to how we should live?

The sense of the opening lines (6:19-21) is clear: Cut your entanglements in material possessions, for since they are subject to loss, they occasion a loss of balance, e.g., an inordinate absorption in security. Later Christian tradition used the word "detachment" for the attitude that Jesus commends. Then in 6:22-23 the speaker makes a different and still more fundamental point: Actions come from the subject of action, whose horizons, perspectives, purposes, and desires determine what the actions will be. If the subject is good, the actions will be good. (We might observe here that the figure of the eye as the lamp of the body supposes a theory of eyesight widely shared in the ancient world: the eye shines, for light from within the body sends out "rays of sight" through the eye, just as sometimes in comic strips or cartoons a character is represented as seeing something by a line and arrow from his eye to the object.)

There follows a return to the theme of detachment (6:24). No slave can serve two masters (God and "wealth," for "Mammon," from the Aramaic word *māmôn/māmônā*," means "possessions, wealth").

Finally, we return to our main question, which concerns 6:25-34. In what sense do the wild birds and lilies teach us how to live? In no sense really, for the question is misleading. The birds and flowers are not models to imitate; rather, the care that God lavishes on the birds and flowers attests his even greater care for us! For the man or woman of faith will spontaneously say, in accord with biblical tradition, "How much more surely must our heavenly Father take care of us!" And

it is just this faith that allows us to moderate what might otherwise become a dominant burden and anxiety, one calculated
to distract us from a far more crucial concern: God's Reign and
righteousness (6:33).

MAIN BODY: PART FOUR, WISE WARNINGS

7:1 Do not condemn, lest there be One to condemn you.

  2 For with the standard of judgment by which you condemn
       there is One who will condemn you,
    And with the measure by which you measure out,
       there is One who will measure out to you.

  3 Why do you see the speck that is in your brother's eye
    and do not notice the log that is in your own?

  4 And how can you say to your brother,
    "Here, let me take the speck out of your eye,"
    when, look! there is a log in your own!

  5 Hypocrite! First take the log out of your own eye
    and then you will see clearly enough
    to take the speck out of your brother's eye.

  6 Do not give what is holy to dogs
    and do not cast pearls before swine,
    for they will only trample them underfoot
    and turn to tear you apart.

  7 Keep asking and it will be given you,
    keep looking and you will find,
    keep knocking and the door will open to you;

  8 for it is the one who keeps asking who receives,
    the one who keeps looking who finds,
    the one who keeps knocking, to whom the door opens.

  9 Is there a man among you who,
    if his son asks him for bread, will give him a stone?

    7:1-2: Divine passives.

    7:6a: Matthew, in the context of instruction against judging and
condemning others, nevertheless urges that discrimination is appropriate: Do not reveal everthing at once to all comers. (In Jesus'
original use, the proverb read as follows: "Put no [precious nose-]
ring on dogs, / and hang not your [strings of] pearls on the snouts
of swine." The general meaning is much the same.)

10 Or, if he asks him for fish, will give him a snake?

11 So, if you, bad as you are, still know enough
to give your children what is good,
how much more shall your heavenly Father
give good things to those who petition him?

12 Whatever, then, you wish people to do to you,
you do to them,
for this is the Law and the prophets.

13 Enter through the narrow gate!
Broad and spacious is the road that leads to destruction
and more numerous are those that enter by it.

14 But the gate is narrow and the road hard that leads to life,
and less numerous are those that find it.

15 Be on guard against false prophets
who come to you in the guise of sheep
but underneath are ravenous wolves.

16 By their fruits you will know them.
Do people pick grapes from thornbushes
or figs from thistles?

17 Just so, a good tree bears good fruit
and a rotten tree rotten fruit.

18 No good tree can bear rotten fruit
and no rotten tree can bear good fruit.

19 Trees that do not bear good fruit
are cut down and burned.

20 So, by their fruits you will know them.

21 Not everyone who says to me, "Lord, Lord"
shall enter the Reign of heaven,
but only those who do the good pleasure of my heavenly
Father.

7:13: "Enter through the narrow gate!" This is a monumental gate, ordinarily a city gate. (Originally the saying said: "Travel by the narrow [mountain-] pass.") The text uses "many" and "few" in a correlative comparative sense: More numerous are those who take the broad and spacious road, less numerous are those who go by the hard road and find the narrow gate. (Jesus' original imagery of the narrow pass/the broad road was coherent; once the "pass" became a "gate," the imagery became somewhat garbled.)

22   Many will say to me, when that Day comes, "Lord, Lord!
         Did we not prophesy in your name,
         and in your name drive out demons,
         and in your name do many wonders?"
23   And then I will solemnly declare to them:
         "I have never known you!
         'Depart from me, all ye workers of iniquity!' "
24 Whoever then listens to these words of mine and does them
         will be like the sensible man who built his house on rock:
25   The rain fell and the floods came
         and the winds blew and beat on that house,
             but it did not fall,
             for its foundations were on rock.
26 And whoever listens to these words of mine and does not do
         them
         will be like the fool who built his house on sand:
27   The rain fell and the floods came
         and the winds blew and beat on that house,
             and it fell—
             and great was its downfall!

Main Thrust

The last part of the speech is a series of admonitions and
warnings. The objects of these admonitions and warnings are:
(a) condemning others; (b) undiscerning speech on sacred
things; (c) need for perseverance in prayer and grounds for
confidence that God will answer prayer; (d) the golden rule;
(e) readiness to take the hard road and to enter by the narrow
gate; (f) alertness and discernment vis-à-vis prophets: by their
fruits you will know them; (g) what counts is not prophecy
but doing the will, the good pleasure, of God; (h) not just
listening to Jesus' words but doing them is what counts for
survival of the (as yet unidentified) test.

7:22: "That Day": the day of the great judgment.
7:23: "Depart from me . . . ": a citation from Ps 6:8.

Sense of the Speech as a Whole

The antitheses summon the disciples not only *to observe* the Torah but *to transcend* it! This grounds indifference to the prestige of piety, and it grounds the joy of freedom from cares. The concluding warnings accent the *practical* decision called for: a new critique, turned not on one's neighbor but on oneself; a new discernment of religious values; and a new determination to be not only a hearer of Jesus' word but a doer of it.

The sermon calls for the boldness and high spirits of one starting out on an adventure. Its ideals are challenging and promise a new and unforeseeable future. Down-to-earth in detail, they appeal to the most authentic impulse in every listener.

Chapter 3

THE MISSIONARY DISCOURSE

(Matthew 10:5–11:1a)

Following the Sermon on the Mount, Matthew presents a series of stories dominated by wonderworking. Though a few non-miracle stories are presented as well, chapters 8 and 9 of the Gospel mainly depict a cascade of miracles: the healing of a leper, of the centurion's servant, of Peter's mother-in-law, of many sick persons at Peter's house; the stilling of a tempest; the exorcism of the Gadarene demoniacs; the healing of a palsied man; the raising of a "ruler's" daughter from the dead; the healing of two blind men and of a dumb demoniac. For Matthew, the Messiah reveals himself above all in the activities of proclaiming, teaching, and healing (Matt 4:23; 9:34). Called to and prepared for his messianic task in chapter 3, Jesus inagurated it by his *proclamation* in chapter 4. This was followed by his *teaching* in chapters 5–7, which in turn was followed by numerous *healings* in chapters 8 and 9. He has inaugurated the great eschatological (i.e., climactic and definitive) program of restoring and saving his people.

Having thus presented the dramatic core of Jesus' messiahship-in-action, Matthew has implicitly raised the question: What was Israel's response? But before he answers this question (in the narrative-and-discourse section that runs from chapter 11 to chapter 13), he had to make it clear that Israel, or at least a large part of Israel, was in a position to respond. Israel must have heard Jesus or heard of him. Hence the present chapter, which narrates the sending out of the disciples.

58

Moreover, here Matthew strategically presents the sovereign messianic process by which Jesus accomplished two things. First, he began the process of bonding his twelve disciples with himself in his specifically messianic activities. Second, he gave rein to his deep and instinctive compassion for the masses of the people, sending his disciples to them all over Galilee ("because they were harassed and helpless, like sheep without a shepherd"—Matt 9:36).

Chapter 10 thus opens with the notice of Jesus' *election* of the Twelve to a special participation in his messianic vocation and mission. Matthew does not say that they immediately caught the full impact of this act of Jesus, summed up in the words "he called to him his twelve disciples and gave them authority over unclean spirits, to cast them out, and to heal every disease and every infirmity" (10:1). But they were on their way. Little by little they would learn the full sense of what they were being called on to do.

The second of the five great speeches, then, is addressed, not to the crowds, but exclusively to the disciples. But we should not forget that this instruction is ultimately for the sheep lacking an authentic shepherd. Implicitly the speech says: The one for whom these men will speak, who himself speaks with authority (7:29; 9:6, 8), having been sent by God (10:40) as his "beloved Son" (3:17) and Servant (3:17; see Isa 42:1), is the messianic Shepherd of Israel.

In biblical tradition the coming restoration of the nation was depicted in extravagant symbol: sovereignty restored, the ten lost tribes returned, the outpouring of God's "spirit," a whole gamut of miraculous blessings pertaining to the messianic age. All these motifs do occur in the Gospel of Matthew, but in a distinctive way, free of stately language and conspicuous theater. Great promises are fulfilled in the manner of everyday history. Furthermore, we have seen that the restoration of Israel in Matthew includes the coming of the Messiah and his messianic proclamation (chs. 1–4), the revelation bringing the Torah to its divinely appointed completion (chs. 5–7), and the messianic cures and exorcisms that both symbolize the renewal of

Israel and pragmatically accomplish it (chs. 8–9). Now, in chapter 10, Matthew adds the gathering of the people of God.

This gathering of the people had already been inaugurated and signified by the call of the disciples; it is now heavily accented by their election as twelve (a microcosmic sign of restored Israel) who are to be sent throughout the land of Galilee to gather the flock (not literally, but exclusively by winning a response of faith and repentance).

There can be little doubt that the speech breaks down into two parts. The first part (10:5-15) is commanded by the theme of the mission to all Galilee; the second part (10:16-42) offers deep and mysterious words on "the cost of discipleship."

The first four verses sketch the whole mission in broad strokes, supplying the data on whom the Twelve are sent to (vv. 5-6), what they are to say (v. 7) and do (v. 8).

Verses 8c-15 tell the disciples "how to do it." This breaks down into two parts. First, verses 8c-10 issue the command: "Take no payment!" The work of salvation is wholly and entirely the gratuitous gift of God. Second, verses 11-15 outline the mission itself: whom to stay with (v. 11) and how to respond to acceptance and rejection (vv. 12-15).

An outline of Part One will accordingly look like this:

I. (10:5-15): The Mission
   a) Mission specified (10:5-8b)
   b) Take no payment! (10:8c-10)
   c) How to operate (10:11-15).

PART ONE: THE MISSION

10:5   **Do not go to the gentiles**
        and enter no town of Samaritans;

The disciples were doubtless sent out in six groups of two (see Mark 6:7). Sending "pairs" was standard Jewish procedure to ensure protection and legitimacy of testimony (Deut 17:6; 19:15). One of the two would be the spokesman (see Acts 14:12).

10:5: "Town of Samaritans": *Polis* must be rendered "town," but the original meaning was "province." (*Medîna'* in Palestinian

6   rather, go only to the lost sheep
     that are the house of Israel.
7   And as you go about, proclaim:
8   "The Reign of heaven is at hand!"
     Cure the sick, raise the dead,
     cleanse the lepers, drive out demons.
     You received without payment,
     give without payment.
9   Take as payment neither gold nor silver,
     nor copper change for your belts,

Aramaic could be used in both senses, though they were usually distinguished by form.) Ruling out gentiles and Samaritans as addressees limited the mission field to Jews of Galilee.

10:6: "Only": Semitic speech often (as here) leaves the intended "only" verbally unexpressed. See Matt 5:46: "For if you love [only] those who love you, what recompense do you deserve?"

"The lost sheep": The first genitive in the phrase "the lost sheep of the house of Israel" is ambiguous. It might refer to "some" as "lost sheep" (those of the house of Israel who are lost sheep) or to "all" as lost sheep (the lost sheep that are the house of Israel). The first sense might draw support from Matt 9:13. But three data impose the second interpretation: (a) the phrase alludes to Jer 50:6, "My people has become a flock of lost sheep"; (b) in the introduction to this speech, Matt 9:36 describes the crowds, clearly representative of Israel, as "harassed and helpless, like sheep without a shepherd"; (c) Matt 10:5 contrasts gentiles and Samaritans with Israel—in principle, with the whole nation of Israel.

10:7: This verse differs from 3:2 (John the Baptist) and 4:17 (Jesus) only for want of the word "repent." The element of difference is insubstantial (since repentance in the Gospel's usage is defined not by return to the Torah but by acceptance of the proclaimed Reign of God); the element of sameness binds all three—the Baptist, Jesus, and the disciples—in a single continuous movement of proclamation.

10:8: These words summarize chapters 8 and 9. Cf. 4:23; 9:35.

10:9: Usually these words are construed as a prohibition of taking along even bare necessities. But if *ktaomai* is made to yield "provide yourselves," i.e., "acquire as payment, earn," then verse 8b, opening a new development, becomes entirely intelligible in context; choice of the word "food" in the revised proverb of verse 10d makes excellent sense; an oddity is dispensed with—the Twelve are no longer sent out on their mission barefoot (an oddity that Luke thought him-

10 nor travel sack, nor a second tunic,
        nor sandals, nor staff.
    "The laborer [however] deserves his food."
11 In whatever town or village you come to,
        look for someone worthy [to receive you]
        and stay with him until your departure.
12 On entering a household
        offer it the salutation [of peace].
13 If the household is worthy of it,
        let your peace be upon it;
    if it is not worthy,
        let your peace return to you.
14 And if anyone is unwilling to welcome you,
        or hear your words,
    leave that house or that town
        and shake off the foot-dust [from your clothes].
15 Amen, I say to you:
    The land of Sodom and Gomorrah will fare better
    on the Day of judgment than shall that town.

Main Thrust

What stands behind the practical instructions that Jesus
gives? There is the conviction: Now is the appointed time! The
proclamation itself is part and parcel of the saving act of God.
Second, it is *God's* work, so human payment is out of the question. Third, there is compassion for the sheep that lack a shep-

---

self bound to accept; see Luke 22:35) but are merely forbidden to take
an extra pair of sandals as recompense for their charismatic activity;
the expression "two tunics" is clarified: the second tunic, like the
second pair of sandals, refers to payment or recompense. The rhetorical order is one of descending value from gold through silver to
copper, from sack through tunic and sandals to staff. Luke 10:7 gives
the proverb in what was probably its original form: "The laborer is
worthy of his hire," i.e., deserves to be paid his wages. Matthew's
change accords with the prohibition of taking payment: the missionaries may, however, accept meals.

10:14: Shaking the foot-dust from one's skirts signifies the breaking off of all community (Neh 5:13; Acts 13:51; 18:6).

herd, but this detracts nothing from the dramatic character of the encounter: salvation and ruin are the stakes. Rejection, far more than an abstract idea, looms as a concrete possibility.

PART TWO: THE COST OF DISCIPLESHIP,
Section One: Persecution

10:16 **Behold, I send you out like sheep amid wolves,**
  so be wise as serpents, yet artless as doves.
  17 **Be on your guard against men:**
  For they will deliver you up to their sanhedrins
  and have you flogged in their synagogues;
  18 **and you will be dragged before governors and kings**
  because of me, to bear witness before them and the
  gentiles.
  19 **When they deliver you up, do not be anxious**
  about how to speak or what to say,
  for there is One who will tell you in that hour
  what you are to say;
  20 **it is not you who will speak,**
  but the Spirit of your Father
  who will speak through you.

10:16a: The solemn and emphatic use of "I" in "I send you out" intimates the same power and authority as Jesus' distinctive use of "amen" followed by a solemn assertion. How persons respond to this power and authority will determine their standing before God. Jesus recurrently strikes this note of authority and its full vindication. The most obvious instance is 10:32-33, but the same judgment factor tacitly pervades every use of the motif of eschatological reversal (10:22, 23, 28, 39, 41, 42).

10:16b: The accent falls on "wise." The disciples are to be wise (i.e, skilled) in carrying out their mission and wise (i.e, wary) in the face of danger and deceit. But, though discerning and resourceful, they are not to let themselves be infected with cunning, much less with duplicity. What they stand for should be transparent.

10:18b: The bearing of witness before gentiles can hardly have referred to the original sending of the disciples to the Jews of Galilee; its reference is to the world mission.

10:19b: Divine passive (Greek text, literally: "what you are to say *will be given to you* in that hour), as in verses 22b, 26 (twice), 28, 30.

21 Brother will deliver up brother (to be condemned) to death,
and the father his child;
"Children will rise (to make accusation) against their parents"
and will have them condemned to death.

22 You will be hated by all
because of me;
but the man who holds out to the end—
there is One who shall save him!

23 When they persecute you in one town
flee to the next;
Amen, I say to you:
Before you have finished going through all the towns in
Israel,
the Son of Man shall come!

24 A disciple is not above his teacher,
nor a slave above his master.

25 It is enough that the disciple be like his teacher
and the slave like his master.
If they have called the master of the house "Beelzebul"
what will they shrink from calling the members of his
household?

10:21: The context of "deliver up" is supplied by the Jewish tribunals of verse 17, where "deliver (up)" signifies handing over to a judge with a view to condemnation to death. The Greek *thanatoun*, which means "to put to death," "to condemn to death," refers here to the act of "causing someone to be condemned to death."

10:23: A famously problematic text, on which some commentary has already been offered above. The supposition of the text is that the disciples are bound to the land of Israel by their commission to proclaim the Reign of God and the mission of Jesus, the truth of his death for the life of Israel and the nations. This word says that the end will be soon: the Son of Man will come, bringing the eschatological tribulation to an end even before these missionaries of the rejected Messiah shall have brought their message to its whole audience, i.e., to every single one of the cities of Israel.

10:24-25a: These four lines are proverbial. Jesus applies this wisdom to the coming situation of rejection and persecution.

10:25b: The scientific etymology of the name Beelzebul is "Prince Ba'al" (Ugaritic *zbl*, "prince," is a title of Ba'al, the Canaanite fertility god). Jesus offers a popular etymology, a word-play splitting the name into *bĕ'el* (Aramaic: "master") and *zĕbûl* (Hebrew: "house") to yield "master of the house" (Greek: *oikodespotēs*).

Main Thrust

It is clear that we have abruptly moved into deep waters. Up to verse 15 we had a historically plausible account of Jesus' sending his untried disciples out to all Galilee, to share in his mission of proclaiming and healing. Suddenly, however, we meet themes permeated with dread and charged with a call to heroism in a situation, not of apathy or indifference, but of extreme hostility. Though our primary interest is in grasping the text in its own terms, some explanatory words are needed here. The common hypothesis is that Matthew has retrojected into his account of the sending out of the disciples a mixture of later sayings (following Jesus' ascertainment of the probability of rejection) that Matthew wanted his readers to apply also to the situation of missionaries engaged in the world mission. This world mission had been inaugurated, according to the Acts of the Apostles (13:1-3), from Antioch (probably the community of the editor of the Greek Gospel of Matthew) in the forties of the first century.

Elements of this view are surely correct. Matthew's readers rightly applied the words of the Master to the missionary Church of their own time. But there is a significant addition to be made. Matthew will show the ominous beginnings of national rejection in chapters 11 and 12; he will dramatize Jesus' turn to his disciples in chapter 13; and in the middle of the narrative block that runs from chapter 14 to chapter 17 (namely, at 16:13-23), he will show Jesus as having inferred the coming rejection and as having taken up a strategy designed to make his mission succeed despite rejection, indeed in and through it! This strategy was to solicit a confession of messianic faith from his disciples, to tell them of the coming rejection, to instruct them on the mystery of a new economy of salvation, one that would take his own death into account and incorporate it into the mission of restoring Israel. Yes, he would die, but he would make his death a ransom for Israel and the nations (Matt 20:28), an expiatory and covenant sacrifice for them (Matt 26:28). These themes would become part of a new mission and message to Israel after his death.

That is what Matt 10:23 refers to. The Jesus of history envisioned the disciples' last missionary effort to Israel in the period after Jesus had been rejected and killed! In the midst of this desperate mission, the Day of the Son of Man—of his resurrection and parousia—would come. In actual history, things worked out differently. The resurrection of Jesus took place almost immediately following his death. The parousia still lies in the future.

However the historians finally explain the sayings-material that we find in Part Two of the missionary discourse, its message in any case is crystal clear: You will meet vicious persecution "because of me." Families will tear themselves apart, as the prophet (Mic 7:6) prophesied. Do not expect an easier lot, for "a disciple is not above his teacher nor a slave above his master."

PART TWO: THE COST OF DISCIPLESHIP,
Section Two: Fearless Witness

10:26 **Do not be afraid of them:**
    Everything covered God will uncover,
      everything hidden he will make known;
  27 **what I tell you in the dark speak out in the light,**
    and what you hear whispered proclaim from the housetops.

10:26b: These words may well have been proverbial, bearing the sense "everything comes to light." But in their present context and use, they affirm that the message of the Reign of God will make its way; nothing will stop or extinguish it. In this applied sense the passives become "divine": God will make sure that the word will be spread. (According to the introduction to the speech, in 9:38, God himself is "Lord of the [missionary] harvest.")

10:27: This verse has long baffled interpreters, since elsewhere Jesus does not command them to take esoteric instruction and convert it into public proclamation. In the mission that we have posited as a hypothesis—namely, in the light of his coming rejection, Jesus commanded his disciples to carry on the messianic mission of proclaiming until the Son of Man should have come—this is precisely what they are commanded to do.

28 Have no fear of those who kill the body
     but cannot kill the soul;
     fear rather One who can destroy
     soul and body both, in the pit.

29 Are not sparrows sold
     two for a penny?
     And yet not one of them
     can fall to the ground
     against your Father's will.

30 Rather, there is One who has counted
     every hair on your heads.

31 So you must not be afraid—
     you are worth more than many sparrows.

32 Everyone who acknowledges me before men
     I in turn will acknowledge before my heavenly Father;

33 but anyone who disowns me before men
     I in turn will disown before my heavenly Father.

34 Do not think that I have come to bring peace on earth;
     I have come to bring not peace but a sword.

35 For I have come to set a man "against his father
     and daughter against mother
     and daughter-in-law against mother-in-law"

36   and "a man's foes will belong to his own household."

37 No one who loves father or mother more than he loves me
     is worthy of me,
     and no one who loves son or daughter more than he loves me
     is worthy of me,

38 and no one who refuses to take up his cross and follow me
     is worthy of me.

10:29: A sparrow is proverbially worthless: two for a penny (Matt 10:29), five for two pennies (Luke 12:6).

10:34-37: Jesus' public mission will end in his rejection, suffering, and death, which will usher into history the "time of the sword," i.e., the Ordeal or tribulation. A harsh aspect of this Ordeal will be the rupture of family ties over Jesus.

10:38: Another image revealing in a flash how Jesus thought of his own destiny as paradigm for the end of time. The advance revelation of the scandal of the rejected Messiah is accompanied by a renewed call to discipleship. The image of "taking up the cross" focuses

39 Whoever finds his life will lose it,
    and whoever loses his life for my sake will find it.
40 Whoever receives you
       receives me,
    and whoever receives me
       receives him who sent me.

Main Thrust

The same dark tone that colored the passage on persecution continues to dominate the passage on "fearless witness."
No task is nobler than the missionary task; no task is more
fraught with drama (for life and death in the deep, maximum
sense of everlasting life and everlasting death are at stake: vv.
32-33, 37-39); no task is more radically involved in forging and
destroying human bonds. For the first time we are told that,
once the messianic herald has come, the deep and decisive issue in human history becomes "the gospel."

That "fearless witness" is the dominant theme is clear, first,
from the context, i.e., instruction to missionaries as they are
about to set out; second, from the explicit announcement in
verse 26 ("Do not be afraid of them"); third, from the recur-
rence of the theme itself in the positive sense of fearless proclamation (the Matthean sense of vv. 26-27, 32-33, 39).

It remains true that no one theme is consistently sustained,
for the second part of the speech is made up of short units of
disparate origin and original context. Nevertheless, three
thematic notes are struck here. The first touches courageous

---

on the moment when the cross-bar is imposed on a condemned man,
who must carry it to the execution site. At that moment he is dis-
owned by society. Are you ready for that? Jesus asks.

10:39 (variants in Mark 8:35 = Luke 9:24; Luke 17:33; Matt 16:25;
John 12:25): These words not only state the messianic mystery but
invite the disciple to enter into it. Eschatological paradox is presented
as entrée into communion with the Messiah.

10:40: The magnitude of the messengers' authority is made explicit by climactic parallelism. (See *parallelism.) In "you," the disciples, they meet *me*; and in me they meet God himself who sends me.

witness to Jesus. This is just what he is sending his disciples out to do. Recompense for courageous witness, whether of the proclaimers or of those who hear and accept their proclamation, will be the decisive witness of the Son of Man in favor of believers at the moment when the world will be judged. The theme of this Son-of-Man saying thus fits perfectly in the missionary discourse. (From a historical point of view, to be sure, it is out of place, for the theme of the Son of Man's role in the parousia and judgment belonged, in all probability, to the latter part of Jesus' ministry, after the messianic confession of Simon in the region of Caesarea Philippi.)

The second thematic note concerns Jesus' task: to launch the eschatological Ordeal! The Ordeal was to be a time of affliction. It had been prophesied by Jeremiah and Daniel. Here Jesus speaks of the Ordeal in an image perhaps drawn from Ezekiel. He says that he has not come to bring peace but a sword. This is akin to the oracle in Ezekiel, ''Let a sword go through the land'' (Ezek 14:17). Jesus fully intended and willed to force a radically divisive decision on Israel, not out of the love of conflict, but because his task was to win a response of faith. (It would not do just to elicit spectator responses of the kind sought in election polls.) His task was to gather the remnant of Israel in the last days.

The third thematic note is the love of Jesus: It must take precedence over every human love! Is this an outrageous demand? In a sense it is. Biblical tradition had known of the demand of God himself for such love. Here the same sort of demand is made by a man! Only time would make the rationale of such extravagance clear. It would turn out to be the most mysterious dimension of Jesus' messiahship: its status as paradigm of entry into life!

PART TWO, Section Three: Reward

10:41 Whoever receives a prophet because he is a prophet
        shall receive a prophet's reward,
        and whoever receives a righteous man because he is a righteous man

> shall receive a righteous man's reward.
>
> 42 And whoever gives to one of these little ones
> so much as a cup of cold water because he is a disciple,
> Amen, I say to you:
> he shall not miss his reward!

Main Thrust

As addressed to the disciples about to start on their mission, the motif of rewards promised to those who receive them accents the greatness of the gift that they are bringing to their listeners: the saving word not merely of the missionary, but that of the messianic Master who sends him, and not merely of the Messiah but of God who has sent the Messiah!

This concluding section, it must be acknowledged, has been only loosely coordinated with the situation of the disciples being sent on their mission. As a pendant to the missionary discourse, it says that not only missionaries but those lesser figures who make up the bulk of the Church and whose task is to receive and to welcome—to heed the prophet, to revere the righteous, and to offer even minimal services to their fellow believers—if they fulfill this task, will not lack their reward.

The Sense of the Discourse as a Whole

The sense of the whole is two-edged. What is happening in the sending out of the Twelve to Galilee? A divine initiative charged with awesome consequence for both Israel and for the disciples is taking place. With the proclamation of the advent of the Reign of God, Israel is offered salvation. Acceptance will bring eternal life; refusal, eternal death (see 11:20-24).

Meanwhile, the disciples as proclaimers are entering into the messianic mystery. Here, too, life and death are peculiarly at stake. To live out their mission in accord with the model of Jesus' own destiny is to lose life and find it. To fall short, to fail, to shrink from the task is to find life—and lose it.

Chapter 4

THE PARABLES DISCOURSE

(Matthew 13:1-53a)

The first ten chapters of the Gospel of Matthew present the initiative of God toward Israel, in and through his Son, Jesus, anointed to accomplish the task of salvation. The initiative, as chapters 11 and 12 emphasize, fulfilled the promises and prophecies and types of the Scriptures; and yet the response of Israel, both to John the Baptist (11:2-19) and to Jesus (11:20–12:50), turned out to be one of refusal and rejection. The parables discourse (13:1-52), by word and act, confirms this, for halfway through the discourse Jesus ceases to address the crowds and turns to his disciples.

This, no doubt, is a stylization of the history of Jesus. We know that he was revered by masses of ordinary people as a prophet, and that among them he prompted the question of just what his role might be in God's plan. Following the fateful act of the cleansing of the temple, his enemies were determined to kill him, but they shrank from arresting him publicly "in the festival crowd" (Matt 26:5). They feared that any such act might trigger a riot.

The Matthean way of streamlining events, particularly the intense focus on the utter scandal of rejection, is an index to Matthean theology. Matthew, of course, shares this focus with other early Christian writers. It stands out strong against the Judaic background. Even if, as some scholars have argued, there was a current of interpretation in Israel that saw the figure of the Messiah in the "Servant" of Isaiah 40–55, whose exaltation followed his suffering and death (Isa 52:13–53:12), no one, either in the pre-Christian traditions of Jewish antiquity or in the scholarship of modernity, has proposed that pre-Christian Israel ever expected, or even entertained the bare notion, that Israel might *reject* its messianic Savior.

The turning point in the story of Jesus' mission to Israel took place beyond the borders of Israel, in sight of Mount Hermon, the region of Caesarea Philippi (the realm of Herod's son Philip until his death in 34 A.D.). There, in view of the rejection of his person and mission that Jesus saw crystallizing in Israel, he drew from his disciples—or, more exactly, from their leader and spokesman, Simon—a confession of messianic faith. He accepted this confession as the divinely graced acknowledgment of the truth of his mission. But Jesus immediately initiated his disciples into an appalling scandal: Israel was about to reject its messianic Savior.

This revelation, which was the central and controlling purpose of the entire Caesarea Philippi episode, came to the disciples as an unbearable paradox. It contradicted the strong, entirely understandable Jewish tendency, which ran like a thread through the whole history of ancient Israel, to "success theology." In the Judaism of the time of Jesus, it was a matter of self-evident supposition that the Messiah, when he would come, could not fail. He could not fail to be acknowledged, and he could not fail in his purposes.

Jesus, too, was fundamentally persuaded that in an ultimate sense he must not and would not fail. The saving act of God would be placed once, and once only, in human history. He was commissioned to see to it, regardless of Israel's response, that that saving act should succeed. The question was, How?

We have seen Jesus' answer, but since it is so frequently overlooked or misconstrued, we shall repeat it. How succeed? By Jesus' not only taking account of refusal but integrating the refusal into his mission. In Jesus' perspective, scriptural and providential necessity called for his mission ultimately to triumph over every obstacle, however real, however formidable, that the Jerusalem establishment might throw in his path: unbelief, hostility, deliberate misunderstanding, conscious repudiation. We are probably well advised to understand Jesus' prophecy of failure in provisional terms. He was aware of deadly hostility, some of it already actual (on the part of the ethnarch Herod Antipas and of the Pharisaic movement), more of it still potential (on the part of the Sadducean temple clergy). Would Israel as a whole follow the lead of these establishment forces? We must assume, on the basis of Jesus' powerful appeal to Israel-on-Passover-pilgrimage (an appeal mounted in and through a symbol-charged entry into Jerusalem and the immediately following cleansing of the temple), that the response of Israel at large was an unanswered question. Both Jesus and the Jerusalem establishment seem to have taken it precisely as an unanswered question.

The climax of the drama would be played out at Passover in the capital city. Jesus himself would set it in motion by the pre-Passover symbolic acts of entering Jerusalem and cleansing the temple. These acts would prompt the conspiracy of his adversaries (Mark 11:18), who were intent on "destroying" Jesus. They had a problem: As a charismatic prophetic figure, Jesus was protected by "the festival crowd" (the meaning of the Greek phrase *en tȩ heortȩ* in Mark 14:2 = Matt 26:5). Judas solved the conspirators' problem by promising to let them know where Jesus would be when he was unprotected by the crowd. So it happened. Jesus was captured at night, in the company of a few disciples only, was tried, found guilty, delivered to the Romans, and executed.

Once Jesus of Nazareth was rejected and condemned by the Sanhedrin and executed by the Roman administration of Judea and Samaria, friend and foe alike found themselves obliged to work out some intelligible interpretation of these events. The foes of Jesus interpreted him after his death, as they had at the end of his life, as a false prophet. He could not have been the Messiah, for, having been hanged on the cross, he was accursed by God (literally, "a curse of God" — Deut 21:23). Those who encountered the Jesus divinely vindi-

cated by his resurrection from the dead not only interpreted
the events in favor of Jesus and to the detriment of his accusers
and enemies, but in various ways they accented the paradox
and scandal of the repudiated Messiah and Savior. Matthew
planned the forward movement of his Gospel narrative as a
whole on the pivotal theme of rejection. (Paul had gone even
further, highlighting that concentrated essence of paradox and
shame, the cross.)

Historically, Jesus had used parables when they were ap-
posite to the follow-up on his proclamation. For example, he
preferred to answer objections and dispel doubts in a way that
led the listener to insight. The intended response to a parable
is a little like the intended response to a joke. Parable and joke
both call for a flash of insight: "I get it!" Jesus supplied images skillfully correlated and let his listeners draw on their own
resources to get to the right conclusion. Led by his or her own
insight, the listener was more likely to adopt the speaker's view
on the issue under discussion. Skill and discretion alike were
at work in the parabolist's images. Nothing was more characteristic of Jesus than this preference for concreteness and indirection.

Those who shaped and transmitted the oral tradition in the
post-Easter Church gathered the parables together, partly to
facilitate memorization. The parables were thus cut off from
their original, quite diverse contexts. Inevitably, how to interpret them became problematic. The solution settled on in the
course of oral tradition was "allegory." Ironically, a brilliant
rhetoric of clarification thus became a rhetoric of mysterious
meaning. A few parables were outfitted with allegorical "explanations," which functioned as models of interpretation. Finally, as heirs of the tradition, the evangelists presented whole
sets of parables in the framework of a single setting. Thus was
born the parables discourse.

In Matthew's Gospel the discourse breaks down into two
parts, sharply distinguished by a change in setting. The first
setting (13:1-35) has Jesus in a boat offshore, addressing the
crowds on the shore. (True, there is an insertion from a later

scene and setting; this kept the parable of the sower and its explanation together, but at the price of a certain awkwardness.) The second setting (13:36-52) places Jesus in a house with the disciples alone.

A first effort to structure chapter 13, therefore, would have the following look:

I. *In the boat* (13:1-35)
　To the crowds (13:1-9)
　　Parable of the sower
　[To the disciples (13:10-23)
　　Why Jesus uses parables for the crowds
　　Explanation of parable of the sower]
　To the crowds (13:24-33)
　　Parable of the tares amid the wheat
　　Parable of the mustard seed
　　Parable of the leaven
　Concluding editorial notice on parables to the crowd

II. *In the house,* to the disciples alone (13:36-52)
　　Explanation of the parable of the tares
　　Parable of the hidden treasure
　　Parable of the pearl of great price
　　Parable of the dragnet and its explanation
　　Mini-parable concluding parables discourse

Is the discourse structured concentrically? Numerous critics think so. Paul Gaechter, counting seven parables in chapter 13, proposed the following structure:[5]

　　1. Parable (13:4-9)
　　　Purpose and Explanation (13:10-23)
　　2. Parable (13:24-30)
　　3. Parable (13:31-32)
　　4. Parable (13:33)
　　　Purpose and Explanation (13:34-43)
　　5. Parable (13:44)

6. Parable (13:45-46)
7. Parable (13:47-50)
   Conclusion (13:51-52).

Gaechter, moreover, was convinced, like others, that there was a concentric structuring of the parables. He thus worked out the following remarkable design:

First parable (13:4-9)

  Second parable (content: division at the end of time)

    Third parable (13:31-32) ⎫

                   ⎬ Paired

    Fourth parable (13:33) ⎭

    Fifth parable (13:44) ⎫

                   ⎬ Paired

    Sixth parable (13:45-46) ⎭

  Seventh parable (content: division at end of time)

Conclusion (13:51-52)

The merit of this proposal is that it takes account of two sets of data possibly relevant to Matthew's design. First, it is true that in terms of thematic context the parable of the mustard seed (third parable, 13:32) and the parable of the leaven (fourth parable, 13:33) are paired; so are the parables of hidden treasure (fifth parable, 13:44) and the pearl of great price (sixth parable, 13:46); and so, finally, are the parables of the tares amid the wheat (second parable, 13:24-30) and the dragnet (seventh parable, 13:47-50). Gaechter's proposal makes sense not only of Matthew's juxtaposing the third and fourth parables, and the fifth and sixth, but also of his separating the second and seventh parables.

Are there any drawbacks to this scheme? Not necessarily, but two observations are in order. First, Gaechter's proposal takes no account of the change of setting that divides the discourse into two parts. This division, however, fits perfectly into his theory of concentric structure. It would, in fact, constitute the exact center—the shift of focus from the crowds to the disciples—around which the rest of the materials are organized. Second, Gaechter's proposal takes no account of the play between parables and explanations or interpretations of parables. Whether this tells against his proposal is not yet clear.

Something of an independent confirmation is provided by the analysis of David Wenham,[6] who does, however, differ from Gaechter in a number of particulars. We shall mention three. First, he counts eight parables rather than seven, giving full parable status to what we have called the "mini-parable" of 13:51-52, and he explicitly correlates the content of the first parable with that of the eighth. Second, he takes account of the change of setting and audience. Third, Wenham offers his own sort of concentric structuring of the beginning and the end of the discourse:

> (a) parable (13:-9)
>   (b) question/answer (13:10-17)
>   (c) interpretation (13:18-23)
>   (c') interpretation (13:49-50)
>   (b') question/answer (13:51)
> (a') parable (13:52).

Both scholars correlate the beginning with the end. Both correlate the tares (13:24-30) with the dragnet (13:47-50). Both take the discourse to pivot on a center that divides two pairs of parables: mustard seed and leaven, hidden treasure and pearl of great price.

How good is the theory of concentric structure? It is probable though not compelling. Admittedly, this is often the best we can expect in issues of literary organization.

THE PARABLES DISCOURSE

PART ONE: IN THE BOAT (13:1-35):
To the Crowds (13:1-9; 24-33)

13:1   That same day Jesus left the house and sat by the lake-
2   side. • There gathered before him crowds so numerous that
he went aboard a boat and sat there, and the whole crowd
3   stayed on the shore. • And he spoke to them of many things
in parables.
4   "A sower went out to sow. • And as he sowed, some seed
5   fell on the path and the birds came and devoured it. • Other
seed fell on rocky ground where there was little soil, and it
6   soon sprang up for lack of soil; • and when the sun rose it
7   was scorched; and having no root, it withered. • Other seed
8   fell on thorns and the thorns grew up and choked it. • Other
seed fell on good soil and brought forth grain, some a hun-
9   dredfold, some sixty, some thirty. • Let him hear who has
ears."
10   [To the disciples, 13:10-23] Then the disciples came to him
11   and said: "Why do you speak to them in parables?" • And
he answered them,

> "There is One who has given to you
> to know the secrets of the Reign of heaven,
> but to them He has not given this.

12   For, to him who has there is One who will give more;
but from him who has not He will take away even what
he has.

In the opening of his parables chapter, Mark says that Jesus began *to teach* (Mark 4). Matthew, by contrast, does not say that he *taught*
the crowds, but only that "he spoke to them of many things in parables." Why? The messianic function of teaching has its implied correlative in learning. But the crowds do not learn!

13:10-12: The question in verse 10 receives its full answer in verses
11-17. Since the passives in the Greek text of verse 11 are "divine
passives" ("has been given" / "has not been given"—namely, by
God), the proverb in verse 12 (an ancient version of "the rich get richer
and the poor get poorer") is used to make a religious point: The way
to blessing is *response* to blessing.

13 This is why I speak to them in parables:
   for, seeing, they do not see,
   and hearing they do not hear, nor do they understand.
14   To their loss the prophecy of Isaiah is fulfilled:
      'You shall indeed hear but not understand
      and you shall indeed see but not perceive.
15   For the heart of this people has grown crass
         and their ears are hard of hearing,
            and their eyes they have closed
               lest they should perceive with their eyes,
            and hear with their ears
         and understand with their heart
         and turn for me to heal them."
16   But blessed are your eyes, for they see,
      and your ears, for they hear.
17   Truly, I say to you
      many of the prophets and of the righteous longed
   to see what you see, and did not see it,
   and to hear what you hear, and did not hear it.

13:13-18: These verses are made up of diverse materials, but Matthew, by disposing the text in concentric fashion (as Nils Wilhelm Lund showed in 1942) gives a pleasing visible and audible unity to the answer of Jesus in these verses.

13:13-15: These verses are controlled by the language of a famous text in the Book of Isaiah on the call and cleansing of Isaiah while he was in the sanctuary building of the temple of Jerusalem (Isa 6:1-7). The terms of Isaiah's mission are made to apply to Jesus.

Note, in accord with the diverse indentations of the text, how the parts are played off against each other (the crowds' failure to see and hear against the disciples' seeing and hearing, and so throughout the whole text). How many times do the words "see" and "hear" appear? Are the repetitions effective? Do these words shape the passage? This probably explains why Matthew connects Jesus' answer to the question of why he speaks to the crowds in parables with his interpretation of the parable of the sower by verse 18, "*Hear*, then, the parable of the sower."

In Mark's Gospel the disciples recurrently misunderstand Jesus; but Matthew has just presented the disciples as blessed by the capacity to see and hear.

18   Hear, then, the parable of the sower.

19   When anyone hears the word of the Reign, and does not un-
20   derstand it, the evil one comes and snatches away what is
sown in his heart: this is what was sown on the path. • As
for what was sown on rocky ground, this is he who hears the
21   word and immediately receives it with joy; • but having no
root in himself, he momentarily holds out, but when tribulation or persecution arises on account of the word, he soon
22   stumbles. • As for what was sown among thorns, this is one
who hears the word, but worldly anxiety and the seduction
23   of riches choke the word, and it remains fruitless. •As for
what was sown on good soil, this is he who hears the word
and understands it; he indeed bears fruit, and yields a hundredfold, or sixtyfold, or thirtyfold.

24   [To the crowds, 24-33] Another parable he put before them,
saying, ''The Reign of heaven is like a man who sowed good

13:24: From verse 34 we must infer that here we are again back to the shore of the Lake of Galilee; again Jesus addresses the crowds from his seat in the boat.

''The Reign of heaven is like a man who . . . '' The word ''like'' is a shortened form of an introductory formula. In the full form (as we learn from rabbinic literature) the introduction runs as follows: ''To what may the matter be compared? To a man, who . . . '' This is shortened and simplified, dropping ''To what may the matter be compared?'' But the short form may mislead the reader. Thus, a purist might translate, using the implied long form: ''It is with the Reign of heaven as with a man who sowed good seed,'' and the hearer would listen for the point of comparison, which is not ''the man who sowed good seed'' but rather the rationale for his decision not to up-root the tares until the harvest. Similarly, the point of comparison in the parable of the mustard seed, despite the words ''The Reign of heaven is like a mustard seed,'' is not the seed itself but the all but miraculous emergence from the tiny seed of the great bush in whose boughs the birds nest.

The reader must accordingly be on the lookout, like any listener to parables, for the point of comparison and should not assume that the formula of introduction makes it available from the start. (Thus, in this text the Reign of God is not ''like a man who sowed good seed,'' but like his decision not to uproot the tares until the harvest. In verse 45 the Reign of God is not ''like a merchant'' but like a pearl.

25 seed in his field; • but while people slept, his enemy came
26 and sowed tares amid the wheat, and went away. • So when
the plants came up and bore grain, then the tares appeared.
27 The servants came to find the householder and said to him,
'Master, was it not good seed that you sowed in your field?
28 How then has it tares?' • He said to them, 'Some enemy has
done this.' The servants said to him, 'Then do you want us
29 to go and gather them?' • But he said, 'No, lest in gathering
30 the tares you root up the wheat along with them. • Let both
grow together until the harvest; and at harvest time I will tell
the reapers, Gather the tares first and bind them in bundles
to be burned, but gather the wheat into my barn.' "
31   Another parable he put before them, saying, "The Reign
of heaven is like a mustard seed which a man took and sowed
32 in his field; • it is the smallest of all seeds, but when it has
grown it is the greatest of shrubs and becomes a tree, so that
the birds of the air come and make nests in its branches."
33   He told them another parable. "The Reign of heaven is
like leaven which a woman took and buried in three measures of meal, so that the whole finally fermented."
34   All this Jesus told the crowds in parables; indeed, he said
35 nothing to them without a parable. • This was to fulfill what
was spoken by the prophet:

In chapter 18, as we shall see, the Reign of God is not "like an earthly
king" but like a settlement of accounts. In chapter 20 it is not "like
a householder" but like a distribution of wages. In chapter 22 it is
not "like a king" but like a marriage feast.)

13:31-33: Matthew intends that his readers interpret each parable
allegorically. In some instances (sower; tares amid the wheat; dragnet) he offers an allegorical explanation of the parable. But there is
no reason to suppose that only one allegorical reading is assigned to
each parable. Matthew had no doubt heard many allegorical interpretations and considered that this only accented the richness of the parables of Jesus as sources of secret and inexhaustible meaning.

Apropos of the salvation of the nations (the birds in the branches)
by assimilation to restored Israel: In Christian history this was first
conceived in literal accord with the post-historical pilgrimage of the
peoples, and later—as in the Acts of the Apostles and, no doubt,
among all the evangelists—as missionary success among gentiles following on missionary success among Jews.

"I will open my mouth in parables,
I will cry out what has been hidden since the foundation
of the world."

Main Thrust

The parables, as the introductory paragraphs to this chapter indicated, came to the evangelists as a rhetoric of mystery: allegories of salvation. The task assigned to parables no longer bound to any concrete context—doubts to be resolved, difficulties to be dismantled—was now straightforwardly didactic: to present deep truths clothed in mystery.

Before we take up the deep truths, why did God see to it that they be clothed in mystery? Part of the answer is that many things are beyond the reach of our understanding. No doubt, the main baffling issue was the unbelief that had met the mission of Jesus in Israel. This strange, scandalous fact—the refusal of faith crystallized in the repudiation of Jesus—must have bewildered the pagans addressed by the world mission. How could it have happened?

The answer given here is that it happened by scriptural necessity, that is, God so willed it. This was not a complete explanation, but it did *locate* the explanation, namely, in the plan of God. At this point Matthew offers no further instruction on the plan of God. Here he first of all invites the reader to hope to be found among those to whom the secret of the Reign of God is given. Second, he implicitly invites the reader to keep alert for further instruction on the destiny of unbelieving Israel. Third, though the matter is proposed as a divine decision, it is to be understood that God's dispositions are not arbitrary. Some failure or fault attaches to the blindness of the "outsiders." Jesus says what it consists in, drawing on figures of blind eyes, deaf ears, a crass heart.

In the coming chapters more light will be shed on this, but without ever wholly dissolving the aura of mystery that clings to the theme of unbelief in the Gospels generally and perhaps most distinctively in Matthew. For the moment the accent falls on the division of believers and unbelievers as a matter of human decision, but with an added emphasis on God's determination to draw good from evil to the benefit of all. The disciples are being taught to acknowledge the prevenient goodness of God: Blessed are your eyes . . . and your ears.

> Truly I say to you
>   many prophets and righteous men longed
> to see what you see, and did not see it,
> and to hear what you hear, and did not hear it.

The issue might be summed up in *election,* a theme prominent in the New Testament but often overlooked today, perhaps because it crosses the grain of many, even most, contemporary mind-sets.

What are the deep truths that the elect are given to grasp? So far as the parable of the sower is concerned, the "explanation" (13:19-23) tells us. The deep truth is the diversity of fruitfulness on the part of those who listen to the word of the Gospel. They are warned, first, to make sure that they are ranged on the side of "good soil." That is: Watch out for the evil one! (Satan, no object of doubt in the time of Jesus, had figured prominently in the previous chapter.) Do not be counted among *the crass,* from whose hearts Satan snatches the word that the Sower had sown. Do not be counted among *the rootless,* who drop out under pressure, nor among *the worldly,* seduced by the worries of the world and a deceptive delight in riches. Remember, even the good soil is diverse. Do not be satisfied with producing grain thirtyfold—no, produce it a hundredfold! We are called to be saints!

As for the deep truth concealed in the figures of the other parables, the evangelist has left it largely up to the reader to figure out what it is in each parable. (Our task is to clarify the writer's sense; where the writer leaves it open to the reader to determine meanings, we shall too.) In Part Two of the parables discourse, Jesus will offer an explanation to the disciples of the parable of the tares amid the wheat.

The parable of the mustard seed, often put under the heading "parables of growth," does indeed strike the note of growth insofar as the great bush comes from the tiny seed. But it may well be that the evangelist, like Jesus himself, intended the accent to fall not on growth but on contrast. (In Jesus' own use of the parable, he accented the contrast between the unimpressive beginnings of his "movement" of eschatological renewal and the impressive destiny of "renewed Israel"—that future moment (the Reign of God) when the great tree of Israel would assume its full stature and give shelter to the birds. The birds nesting in the tree were most probably an image of salvation for the gentiles: if the subject is "birds," the predicate may mean "make nests," but it also has the more general sense of "take shelter." It is used in post-Old Testament Jewish literature to refer to the salvation of the gentiles, e.g., "Joseph and Aseneth," 15:6.) What meaning did Matthew assign to the parable? The question remains open. He may well have applied the image of greatness emergent from small beginnings in one way or another to the life of the Church.

The parable of the leaven is an all but perfect parallel. As the tiny seed yields to the great tree, here a tiny morsel of leaven leavens the great mass of dough. The "three measures" of meal (see Gen 18:6), once leavened, would produce bread for a hundred persons. The woman works it into dough, covers the dough with a cloth, and leaves it to stand overnight. As the tall bush from the tiny seed is a wonder of nature, so the impact of the leaven, visible the next morning, is a wonder of ordinary life.

In the formula of conclusion Jesus cites Ps 77:2. Matthew conceives of Jesus' teaching in parables as itself a fulfillment of Scripture. This corresponds to the Judaic mentality of the time, which tended to read the Scriptures as prophecy, even though a modern, historical-critical reading of many of these texts would not confirm that the original writer intended a *prophetic* sense bearing on messianic salvation in the last days.

To what does the phrase in the editorial notice, "what has

been hidden since the foundation of the world," refer? Whatever Matthew's exact meaning, it must tie in with the parables theory expressed in 13:10-17. It will accordingly be the *secrets of the end-time.* These include the presence of the saving Reign of God in the person and work of Jesus (see vv. 16-17); the coming of Jesus not only to plant the seed of salvation (the word of God) but to judge the world in the future (parable of the tares amid the wheat); the salvation of the nations by assimilation to the saved community of Israel (parable of the mustard seed).

PART TWO: IN THE HOUSE (13:36-52):
To the Disciples Alone

13:36   Then he left the crowds and went home. And his disciples came to him, saying, "Explain to us the parable of the tares
37   of the field." • He answered, "He who sows the good seed
38   is the Son of Man; • the field is the world and the good seed means the sons of the Reign; the tares are the sons of the evil
39   one, • and the enemy who sowed them is the devil; the har-
40   vest is the close of the age, and the reapers are angels. • Just as the tares are gathered and burned with fire, so will it be
41   at the close of the age. • The Son of Man will send his angels and they will gather out of his kingdom all causes of sin and
42   all evildoers, • and throw them into the furnace of fire; there
43   men will weep and gnash their teeth. • Then the righteous will shine like the sun in the Reign of their Father. He who has ears let him hear.

13:36-43: Does the parable deal with evildoers among members of the Church, as many experts, both Catholic and non-Catholic, in the ancient Church, in medieval times, down to the present, have maintained? Perhaps so. As a close parallel to the parable of the tares amid the wheat, the parable of the dragnet suggests that the problem arises as the result of missionary effort. On the other hand, it is possible that the two parables are not perfectly parallel. Verse 38 defines "the field" as *the world.* This might signify that the parable deals rather with another age-old question: Why does God allow vicious sinners to subsist and prosper rather than root them out by judgment?

44   "The Reign of heaven is like treasure hidden in a field,
which a man, having found it, covered up again; then in his
joy he went off to sell all he had and he bought that field.

45   "Again, the Reign of heaven is like a merchant in search
46 of fine pearls, • who, on finding one pearl of great price, went
off to sell all he had and bought it.

47   "Again, the Reign of heaven is like a net which was
48 thrown into the sea and gathered fish of every kind; • once
it was full, men drew it ashore and sat down and sorted the
49 good into baskets but threw away the bad. • So it will be at
the close of the age. The angels will come forward and sepa-
50 rate the evil from the righteous • and throw them into the
furnace of fire; there men will weep and gnash their teeth.

51   "Have you understood all this?" They said to him, "Yes."
52 And he said to them, "Therefore every scribe who has been
trained for the Reign of heaven is like a householder who
brings out of his treasure what is new and what is old."

13:44: People would bury their valuables in times of trouble, e.g.,
invasion. If the owner died before recovering the buried treasure, it
would remain in the ground until someone came upon it. The center
of gravity in this parable is the answer to questions about Jesus' disciples. What was the secret of their contentment and joy? Why were
they so willing to leave all and follow him?

13:45-46: In the ancient world the two most valuable material
items were gold and pearls. What does the pearl stand for here?

13:47-50: "Fish of every kind": The image suggests that the world
mission brings to the Church all sorts, and that not all live lives worthy of the Christian vocation. The Church is meant to be a Church
of saints, but until judgment day it is a Church of saints and sinners.
(Indeed, this was the interpretative line taken by St. *Augustine
against the *Donatists, who wished to posit a Church of saints only.)

13:52: Jesus himself is the model of the apocalyptic scribe who
has become a disciple of the Reign of heaven. Above, he has given
his teaching on the Reign of God in seven different forms.

The meaning of "old and new" depends on the sense of "scribe."
This passage is unique in using "scribe" as a term for a Christian
who, having become a disciple of the Reign of heaven, has entered
into an understanding of its secrets. Out of this understanding heart
and mind he brings forth not only the old (perhaps an allusion to

Main Thrust

Chapters 11 and 12 of Matthew's Gospel depicted the responses of Israel to John the Baptist and to Jesus, opening with the response of the Baptist himself to Jesus and Jesus' words on the Baptist. Then, in the parables discourse of chapter 13, Matthew dramatically deals with why Jesus addresses the crowds in parables. First, "in parables" is made to mean "in a coded and mysterious language." Why? Because that is God's own design. Jesus simply acts in accord with it. (We are not yet told what the designs of God hold in store for the crowds.) Following Jesus' words to the crowds, a scriptural citation defines them as prophecy fulfilled.

Now Jesus addresses his disciples, explaining the meaning of his parables and addressing certain parables peculiarly revelant to the disciples' lives. We thus meet Matthew's crucial differentiation of audiences, equivalent to the Markan distinction between "outsiders" and "you" (Mark 4:11). Can we assign good reasons accounting for Matthew's choice of material for these audiences? We can, for it is enough to explain why certain materials were reserved to the second part of the speech.

This material comes under two headings: the secrets of the end-time (explanation of the parable of the tares amid the wheat, parable of the dragnet, with its explanation) and the theme of joyous discipleship (the hidden treasure and the pearl of great price). Both headings are perfectly comprehensible as properly reserved to this audience, the nucleus of the Church to be. As for the material in Part One of the discourse, the relevant observation is that Jesus here affirms and explains his mission, but the crowds hear only the words, failing to penetrate their meaning.

---

the natural imagery and common lore that we find brilliantly illustrated in the parables discourse) but also the new, spiritual meanings that this imagery and lore have been made to mediate.

The Sense of the Parables Discourse as a Whole

As heir to collections of parables, it was either Mark or Matthew who devised the theology of the parables found in both. In Matthew, in any case, this theology, of which Israel's rejection of Jesus constitutes the pivotal point, has had an impact on the organization of the Gospel narrative as a whole. It sets the tone of the story, beginning midway through the missionary discourse of chapter 10; it dominates chapters 11 and 12; it reaches a crucial point in the middle of the parables discourse; and it peaks with Jesus' revelation to the disciples, following Simon's confession of faith in Jesus as "the Messiah, Son of the living God" (16:16), that the Sanhedrin was about to repudiate Israel's messianic Savior (16:21).

Indeed, it would be in the Caesarea Philippi passages (16:13-23) that the contrapuntal themes of the messianic restoration of Israel and the rejection of the Messiah would coalesce. Both themes had contributed to the organization of the story. Here they dramatically collide. The shift from the addressing of parables to the crowds to the revelation of their secret meaning to the disciples in the middle of chapter 13 prepares the way for this collision. The parables discourse is designed to contribute effectively to this development.

Though the tone is accordingly dark, it is a matter of interest that the discourse concludes on a note of joy and light: the happiness of the disciple, who in Jesus and his mission has found a buried treasure and a pearl of great price, and the deep solace of the evangelist himself, whose voice is heard more clearly than usual in the conclusion to the discourse. It is the voice of the scribe who, having learned the secrets of the Reign of God, serves his community of fellow believers with confident assurance.

Chapter 5

THE ECCLESIAL DISCOURSE

(Matthew 18:1–19:1a)

The narrative material of chapters 14–17 is dominated by the theme of the Church. The plan and purpose of Jesus had been to bring all Israel to its appointed destiny of eschatological restoration. By one of the tragic ironies of history, Israel as a whole, following the line taken by the Jerusalem establishment, turned down the gift of restoration when it was offered. Allusion to "the theme of the Church" as dominating chapters 14–17 comes down, concretely, to a focus on the part of Israel that accepted the gift when it was offered. In the Greek translation of the Scriptures of Israel (third to second century B.C.), the word *ekklēsia* (Church) is the equivalent of the Hebrew word *qāhāl*, the "assembly" of God's own people.

Jesus conceived the work of salvation as the definitive renewal of this *qāhāl*. In Matt 16:18, just after eliciting Simon's messianic confession, he evoked this renewal of the *qāhāl* of Israel in a classic messianic image: the temple or sanctuary that the Messiah was chosen to build (2 Sam 7:13-14 = 1 Chr 17:12-13; cf. Hag 2:20-23; Zech 6:12-13).

According to Judaic tradition, the temple—whether the temple of history or of the coming time of restoration—was built, or was to be built, on the cosmic rock/mountain at the center of the earth, which symbolically epitomized the world's landmass (a mountainous disk surrounded by water). It was also the lid over the netherworld with its subterranean waters.

In Matt 16:18 the image of "the temple" is merely implied in
ekklēsia, but this implied image symbolized, as the explicit word
referred to, the restored people. Jesus assigned the role of foundation for this temple, i.e., the cosmic rock on which the temple
was to be built, to the faith-confessing Simon, who accordingly
was now named "Rock" (in Aramaic *Kêphā'*, which was trans-
literated into Greek as *Kēphas* [English: Cephas] and was translated into Greek as *Petros* [English: Peter]). The netherworld
beneath the cosmic rock, symbolizing the powers of evil and
death, would rage in vain against rock and temple.

Above (p. 20) we saw that the scene of Simon's confession was only one of many narratives in chapters 14–17 to be
dominated by the theme of the Church. Hence, the discourse
on the Church in chapter 18 comes as no surprise. Its compo-
nents (sayings on greatness in the Reign of heaven; parable
of the lost sheep; words on reproving one's brother; themes
of "togetherness" and "reconciliation" linked by catchwords;
parable of the unmerciful servant) were words of Jesus derived from diverse contexts. Here Matthew has firmly shaped
them into a thematically coherent speech of instruction on the
Church.

The most crucial interpretative question is: Who are the real
addressees of the speech? In 18:1 "the disciples" pose the question about "the greatest in the Reign of heaven"; the entire
speech is Jesus' answer. Do "the disciples" here stand for the
whole Christian community? Or do they stand specifically for
Church leaders? Both alternatives can lay claim to a certain
probability, but most New Testament experts today have opted
for the first alternative.

The experts, it would seem, are almost certainly mistaken.
The critical clue to the appropriate answer is the image of the
shepherd in 18:12-14. The term "shepherd" is not applied to
ordinary believers anywhere in the New Testament. In accord
with the well-established usage of the term in the ancient Near
East, in the Old Testament, and in Palestinian Judaism, all New
Testament writers apply the shepherd image, not to believers
in general—who are, rather, "the flock"—but to Church
leaders.

"Shepherds" are usually the leaders of the local Church: "elders" in 1 Pet 5:1 and Acts 20:17; "overseers" or "guardians" or "bishops" in Acts 20:28; "the bishop" in the letters of Ignatius of Antioch to the Philadelphians (2:1) and Romans (9:1). In the Gospel of John (21:15-17), Peter is "shepherd" with respect to the Church as a whole. New Testament texts often spell out concretely the tasks of shepherds, and they are always the tasks of Church leaders.

Once this critical point is established, we find considerable light thrown on the speech both as a whole and in all its parts. A clear specification of addressees from the outset helps us to sharpen the outline of the speech and its thematic progression. A neutral disposition of the materials might be set out as follows:

18:1-4   Paradoxical model: the child
18:5-6   Protecting, not subverting, the faith of children
18:7-10   Sayings on scandals (= inducements to sin) and on "little ones"; [v. 11 spurious]
18:12-14 Parable of lost sheep
18:15-18 Reproving one's brother, binding and loosing
18:19-22 Virtues of togetherness, reconciliation
18:23-35 Parable of the unmerciful servant [Conclusion formula in 19:1a]

Once we hold the key to the intended addressees of the speech, the outline takes on a quite intelligible shape:

18:1-4   A model for Church leaders
18:5-9   Toward the "little ones": a protective ministry
18:10-14 Toward dropouts: an unremitting ministry
18:15-18 Toward the difficult: a ministry of flexible response
          [18:19-20: sayings added on a catchword basis]
18:21-35 Toward offenders: a forgiving ministry.

The interpretation of the Gospels has always been burdened by a peculiar difficulty: how to deal with sayings of Jesus about the future. The present speech is one great saying about the future life of the Church between the resurrection of Jesus and his second coming, or parousia. But there is a difficulty here: Jesus did not anticipate the future precisely as it unfolded; rather, he grasped it in the prophetic manner, symbolically. And in his symbolic scheme of the future, there was no interim between resurrection and parousia. It may accordingly not be amiss to take explicit account of this issue and deal with it here.

Historically, Jesus' anticipation of the future was much like that of the prophets of the Old Testament, who did not foresee the future in its concrete particularity but always as symbols related to one another in a scheme of symbolic time. Thus, the prophets did not speak of divine interventions in the distant future (all such purported "prophecies" are retrojections into the past, outfitted as prophecies by a later writer. See *Apocalypse.). No, the prophets, when they dealt with the future, did so symbolically, and they invariably presented this symbolized future as imminent. (The heirs and readers of the prophets were often puzzled, but apparently not distressed, by the regular failure of prophecy to be followed by immediate realization.)

In Jesus' prophetic scenario, "now" was the moment of his public ministry; "the future" was made up of two periods: that of the Ordeal and that of the Reign of God. The distinction between them was to be established by events (represented below by a vertical line): first, Jesus' repudiation, suffering, and death would introduce the Ordeal; second, "the Day of the Son of Man" (which symbolically included resurrection, messianic investiture, parousia, and judgment) would introduce the Reign of God.

1. Repudiation, suffering,	1	2	
death of Jesus	NOW	ORDEAL	REIGN OF GOD
2. Day of the Son of Man			

Jesus (in the imagery of flock, family, temple, etc.) spoke
of the Church *in the present*, in *the historical future* of the Ordeal, and in *the post-historical future* of the Reign of God. To
summarize Jesus' words: He encourages the Church in the
present, for despite the harsh times coming in the Ordeal, it
will survive the Ordeal and be glorified with Jesus himself, on
the Day of the Son of Man and the coming of the Reign of God.
Some examples: "On this rock (Simon Peter) *I will to build*
[Aramaic substratum] my Church, and the gates of Hades will
not prevail against it" (Matt 16:18). Here Jesus builds his
temple in the present and promises that rock and temple alike
(or Peter and the Church) will not fall victim to the Ordeal,
despite the assaults of Hades (the powers of evil and death).
Again, "Do not be afraid, little flock . . . ," says Jesus (Luke
12:32). The reason why the little flock is not to be afraid is that
it is destined for a brilliant future: "it has pleased your Father
to give you the kingship" (in the future, when the Son of Man
comes—so fulfilling Dan 7:22). What we do *not* find among the
prophetic and symbolic words deriving from the historical Jesus
is *a literal preview* of the future that actually unfolded under
God's sovereign lordship of history. The prophetic scenario
of Jesus, like that of all the prophets, was symbolic. The Church
translates the symbols into the non-symbolic realities that the
symbols refer to. An example of this process of translation:
Matthew's presentation of the ecclesial discourse.

A Model for Church Leaders

18:1   **At that moment the disciples approached Jesus and asked,**
2   **"Who is the greatest in the Reign of heaven?"** • **And calling**

The question of "the greatest in the Reign of God / of heaven"
was apparently recurrent among the disciples (see 20:20-28). Matthew
seizes on it, making it the occasion for Jesus' defining the proper exercise of authority in the Church. Paradox was typical of Jesus, his
mission, and his personal style; here paradox is the norm for his disciples. The model of "greatness" is a little child.

3   to him a little child, he set him before them, • and said,
    "Truly, I say to you, unless you again become like children,
4   you will not enter the Reign of heaven. • Whoever makes him-
    self little, like this child, he is the greatest in the Reign of
    heaven."

Main Thrust

By the sharpest possible contrast with leadership in the
world, leadership in the Church is to be characterized by self-
abasement. In the ecclesial discourse it is not Jesus himself but
a little child (Jewish antiquity, like the rest of the ancient world,
had an unsentimental estimate of children as being of minimal social importance) who is presented as a paradigm of the
lowliness appropriate to Church leaders. Elsewhere in Matthew, Jesus is the model (e.g., Matt 20:20-28), and the thrust
is the same. Whoever aspires to greatness in the Reign of
heaven must choose the way, not of using others and subjugat-
ing them to himself, but of self-forgetful service. The leader
is a lowly servant of the Church.

Toward the "Little Ones": A Protective Ministry

18:5   "Whoever receives those like this little child in my name,
6   receives me. • But whoever induces one of these little ones
    who believe in me to sin, it would be better for him to have
    a great millstone fastened round his neck and to be drowned
    in the depth of the sea.

18:3: "Unless you *again* become like children . . . " This is a
reflection of Semitic idiom. It may be, however, that Matthew intends
the reader to read the idiom literally: "Unless you *turn* and become
like children . . . " In Judaism, repentance was a return to the Law;
in Jesus' mission, repentance was the act of accepting the Reign of
God in the manner of the unpretentious lowly, like a child. Here,
however, the "turn" of repentance is a change of conduct in accord
with a new principle. To be "great" is to make oneself "little."

18:5: "In my name": "For my sake." The expression is practi-
cally equivalent to "because he is my follower."

18:6: Jesus' favoritism toward "the little ones" stands in the Old
Testament tradition of "the poor." The prophets, especially from the

7   "Woe to the world for its inducements to sin! For it is inevitable that such inducements come, but woe to him through
8   whom the inducement to sin comes! • And if your hand or your foot leads you to sin, cut it off and throw it from you; it is better for you to enter life maimed than with two hands
9   or two feet to be thrown into the eternal fire. • And if your eye leads you to sin, pluck it out and throw it from you; it is better for you to enter life with one eye than with two eyes to be thrown into the hell of fire."

Main Thrust

In the time of Jesus' ministry the expression "the little ones" was used of the socially unimportant, e.g., depressed classes such as the destitute and disabled, women and children, the uneducated "simple," and the like. Jesus was conspicuous for his positive attitude toward, and care of, these individuals and groups. In the early Church "the little ones" were especially those who in their simplicity might easily be led astray and "made to stumble." The first item of instruction is alertness to, and care for, these little ones. Here is a point at which the comportment of Jesus and that of Paul strikingly converge. Paul was a model of alertness and care (see 1 Cor 8:7-13; Rom 14:13-23; 15:1-3).

Toward Dropouts: An Unremitting Ministry

18:10   **"See that you do not despise a single one of these little ones; for I tell you that in heaven their angels always behold the face of my heavenly Father. [Omit verse 11.]**

---

period of the Babylonian Exile (6th century B.C.), presented "the poor" and "the afflicted" as the favorites of God. Hence this harsh warning against leading them astray.

    18:7-9: A different angle: the relative weight of physical and moral loss.

    18:10: An easily assumed but badly mistaken attitude toward the little ones. Paul in Rom 12:16 puts it in positive terms: "Do not be haughty, but associate with the lowly."

12   "What do you think? If a man has a hundred sheep and
        one of them has gone astray, does he not leave the ninety-
        nine on the hills to go in search of the one that went astray?
13   And if he finds it—truly, I say to you, he rejoices over it more
14   than over the ninety-nine that did not go astray. • So, it is
        the will of my heavenly Father that not one of these little ones
        should perish."

Main Thrust

The Church leader is to be a shepherd ready to expend
every effort on behalf of sheep gone astray. Here the Matthean
application of shepherd imagery suggests that the parable concerns "dropouts." Church leaders are not to wash their hands
of them, but to set out with determination and patience to win
them back.

Toward the Difficult: A Ministry of Flexible Response

18:15   "If your brother sins against you, go and tell him his fault,
        between you and him alone. If he listens to you, you will
16   have gained your brother. • If he does not listen, take one
        or two others along with you, 'that every word be confirmed
17   by the evidence of two or three witnesses.' • If he refuses
        to listen to them, tell it to the Church; and if he refuses to
        listen even to the Church, let him be to you as a gentile and

-----

18:12-14: Originally Jesus addressed the parable of the lost sheep
to critics stunned by his openness and initiatives toward notorious
sinners. But Matthew has changed the addressees and the main meaning alike. The addressees are the Twelve as shepherds of the Church;
the lost sheep is not a sinner being won over but a believer who has
abandoned the Church. The accent among the images in the parable
changes accordingly from the shepherd's joy at finding the lost sheep
(see Luke 15:5-7) to an earlier moment: the shepherd's determined
persistence in seeking out the straggler.

18:15-17: These verses probably reflect a pre-Matthean manual
for leaders of some Palestinian community of Christians or for the
community at large. There is a parallel in the Essene *Manual of Dis-
cipline* (1QS 5:24b–6:1):

18 a toll-collector. • Truly, I say to you, whatever you bind on
   earth heaven shall bind, and whatever you loose on earth,
   heaven shall loose.
19 "Again I say to you, if two of you agree on earth about
   anything they ask, they will obtain it from my heavenly Fa-
20 ther. • For where two or three are gathered for my sake, there
   am I in the midst of them."

Main Thrust

How are the stubborn to be dealt with? There is no ideal
here of harshly effective authority. The exercise of authority,
rather, is tempered, no stricter than it need be. Excommuni-
cation is a last resort, reserved for the incorrigibly stubborn.
Here, "binding" and "loosing" refer to accepting into and ex-
cluding from the community. Is it the community as a whole
that bears this power? Verse 17 would seem to point in this
direction, but this can hardly be Matthew's intention, for, as
verses 12-14 indicate, the speech as a whole is addressed to
the Twelve precisely in their function as shepherds of the flock
(see Titus 3:10).

Verses 19 and 20 occur here owing to *catchword composition. The catchwords are "on earth" (v. 18) and "in heaven"

They shall rebuke one another in truth, humility, and charity.
Let no man address his companion with anger, or ill-temper,
or obduracy, or with envy prompted by the spirit of wicked-
ness. Let him not hate him [because of his uncircumcised] heart,
but let him rebuke him on the very same day, lest he incur guilt
because of him. And furthermore, let no man accuse his companion before the Congregation without having first ad-
monished him in the presence of witnesses (Geza Vermes, *The
Dead Sea Scrolls in English* [Harmondsworth: Penguin, 1977] 80).

The difficult can be won over; expulsion from the community should
be a last resort.

18:16: Deut 19:15.

18:18: But the Twelve (and in Matthew's day their successors)
do have the authority to expel from the community. "Heaven shall
bind . . . shall loose": translating in accord with Aramaic substratum.

(v. 18 in the Greek text), both of which show up in a different
sense in verse 19; the "two or three" in verse 20 is a reprise
of "two of you" in verse 19 (see also "one or two others" in
v. 16).

Toward Offenders: A Forgiving Ministry

18:21   Then Peter came forward, saying to him, "Lord, if one of
          my brothers sins against me, how often shall I forgive him?
   22   As many as seven times?" • Jesus said to him, "I do not say
          to you seven times, but seventy-times-seven times.
   23   "Thus, the Reign of heaven is like a king who wished to
   24   settle accounts with his servants. • To begin, one was brought
   25   to him who owed him ten thousand talents; • and, as he could
          not pay, his lord ordered him to be sold, with his wife and
   26   children and all that he had, and payment be made. • Then
          the servant falling prostrate, implored him, 'Lord, have pa-
   27   tience with me, and I will pay you everything.' • And,
          touched with pity for him, the lord of that servant released
   28   him and forgave him the debt. • But as he went out, that ser-
          vant came upon one of his fellow servants who owed him
          a hundred denarii; and seizing him by the throat he said, 'Pay

---

18:21-22: Jesus' teaching on forgiveness has only the vaguest fore-
shadowings in the Old Testament; it is distinctive, original.

18:23 See p. 80 on how introductory formulas of parables work.
The Reign of heaven is not like a king but like a settlement of accounts.

The following details on the parable derive from Joachim Jeremias,
The Parables of Jesus (New York: Scribner, 1963).

18:24: "One was brought to him," namely, out of prison. Compare verse 27, where the king "released" him. "Ten thousand talents": a fabulous sum. In the New Testament, "thousands" is the
highest number referred to, and "the talent" is the largest unit of
currency in use in the ancient Near East. The point of referring to
so huge a sum is to underscore the contrast with the trifling debt of
a hundred denarii.

18:25: He had been arrested to preclude flight; now the settling
of accounts was to take place. First, his lands and property were to
be sold. (The parable supposes that the king and other *dramatis perso-
nae* are gentiles; among numerous points that prove this, there is the
fact that in Jewish law the sale of a wife was absolutely forbidden.)

29 what you owe.' • Falling prostrate, his fellow servant be-
    sought him, 'Have patience with me and I will pay you.'
30 But he was unwilling; rather, he had him put in prison till
31 he should pay the debt. • When his fellow servants saw what
    had taken place, they were very distressed; so they reported
32 to their lord all that had taken place. • Then his lord had him
    summoned and said to him, 'You wicked servant! I forgave
33 you all that debt because you besought me; • and should not
    you have taken pity on your fellow servant, as I took pity
34 on you?' • And in anger his lord delivered him to the tor-
35 turers, till he should pay his whole debt. • Thus will my
    heavenly Father do to each of you, if you do not forgive your
    brother from the heart.''

Main Thrust

The speech reaches its climax in the theme of forgiveness:
God has forgiven us, so we should forgive one another. How
graphically the mini-drama of the parable underlines this seem-
ingly simple truth! It is worth noting that this theme, which
touches all, is the high point of an instruction to community
leaders. There will be times when others will offend you, but
forgive them. Forgive them from the heart! Forgive them again
and again!

The Sense of the Speech as a Whole

It is significant that there should exist in the Gospel a speech
of Jesus calculated to meet the inevitable temptation of Church
leaders to lapse, in the course of their service, into abuses of

---

18:29: A minor official for whom the payment of even a small
debt was difficult.

18:31: The ''fellow servants'' were not common slaves but other
high officials.

One aspect of judgment that stands out in the parable is the mercy
shown. This is a development beyond standard Judaic teaching, according to which it is too late for mercy at the judgment. The implied
teaching of the parable is that God will show mercy at the judgment
to those who have shown mercy to others.

authority typical of the world. Even in the Church "status" can be heady, like a potent drink. All the more reason for leaders, remembering that they are called on to serve, to take their cue from the child, paradigm of lowliness. As a narrative of the past, the speech belongs to the esoteric tradition of private instruction of the disciples. At the same time, the speech instructs Church leaders in the present as to how to deal with those who have been entrusted to their care.

The structure of the speech is straightforward. First Jesus sets a child before the disciples—the epitome of the "lowliness" that ought to typify their behavior toward those whom they have been called to serve. Then they are given an instruction on how to deal with four types of subjects: the "little ones," the dropouts, the difficult, and the offenders.

Toward the little ones, simple and unsophisticated: Be most careful not to lead those who lack resources of independence to fall into sin. Toward the dropouts: Do not give up on them! Go in search of them, the way a shepherd searches out the straggler missing among his sheep! Toward the difficult: Be flexible. The less use of power, the better. Only the utterly refractory should be excluded from the communion of the Church. Lastly, toward those who offend: Be boundlessly forgiving from the heart.

Chapter 6

THE ESCHATOLOGICAL DISCOURSE

(Matthew 24:1–26:1a)

The narratives that follow the eschatological discourse and conclude the Gospel of Matthew provide all the elements requisite for understanding Jesus and his mission. A true grasp of his words, including the words that make up this discourse, calls for a true grasp of his mission. A key issue on the mission is raised by the conspiracy of his enemies, leaders of the Jerusalem establishment. They set out to destroy both him and his credibility. Two questions arise: Why? And what was Jesus' response to this?

Matthew does not offer a fully developed view of the "why" question, but he does offer a clue: Pilate, he said, knew that it was out of *phthonos* that the establishment leaders had handed Jesus over to him to be condemned (Matt 27:18). What was this *phthonos*? Usually translated by "envy" or "malice," it may have an even better equivalent in the term that Friedrich Nietzsche and Max Scheler analyzed: *ressentiment*. This is the product of a clash with someone else's values. The someone else is in some uncanny way superior, physically or intellectually or morally or spiritually. The result of the clash is a feeling of hostility that, though perhaps long suppressed and expressed only as a constant belittling of the value in question, may erupt in violence against whoever possesses that value-quality. This is the kind of hostility that may well have had a grip on at least some of the conspirators against Jesus.

Aware of hardening opposition and the prospect of rejection, Jesus undertook to secure the ultimate success of his mission by incorporating this rejection into his own plans. He did this mainly by forming and articulating intentions bearing on his own death. Indeed, he formed these intentions out of what he took to be obedience to the will of his Father, the ultimate author of his mission. In accord with his Father's will, he would die (a) as a "ransom" (Matt 20:28 = Mark 10:45) for Israel and the world (see Isa 43:3-4; 53:10-12); (b) as an expiatory offering (Matt 26:28 = Mark 14:24) for Israel and the world (Isa 52:13–53:12); (c) as a covenant sacrifice (Matt 26:28 = Mark 14:24; see Exod 24:8) sealing a new covenant (Jer 31:31-33) on behalf of Israel and the world (Isa 53:10-12). The blood of the covenant sacrifice itself had expiatory value (see *Tg. Onq.* and *Tg. Ps. Jon.* on Exod 24:8).

Jesus counted on his Father for the realization of a scenario of vindication that would include resurrection, messianic investiture, parousia, and judgment. The last words of Jesus that Matthew recorded prior to the eschatological discourse (Matt 24–25) were "I tell you, you shall not see me again until you say: 'Blessed is he who comes in the name of the Lord' " (Matt 23:39). These words should be related to the scenario of vindication. They belong to the future. What future? Not to the historical future, and especially not to the historical future of the entry into Jerusalem, for that event had already taken place (in Matt 21), but to the parousiac future. It should be noticed that the words are not paralleled elsewhere in the Gospels. They are paralleled, rather, by "the secret" that Paul revealed toward the end of his letter to the Christians of Rome (Rom 11:26): at the parousia "God will save all Israel"!

In a sense we have come a long way from the opening of the Gospel of Matthew, with its accent on proclaiming, teaching, and healing. Jesus' saving act, and Matthew's presentation of it, has taken on a certain complexity. The complexity consists in this: Whereas the primary structure of the mission was its proclaiming and mediating of the Reign of God and restoration of Israel, this has now been overlaid by a secondary structure taking account of, and responding to, Israel's prospective rejection of Jesus. Here "secondary structure" refers to the act that brought the mission of Jesus to concrete realization. It consisted in his dedicating his death, in the sight of God and his disciples, to save the world as "ransom" and "sacrifice."

Finally, we must never forget the future facet of Jesus' mission: Israel at last will greet him with the acclamation "Blessed is he who comes in the name of the Lord." For Matthew, then, the life of the Church was lived, is still being lived, and will be lived within the compass of Jesus' mission. Meantime, he has promised to be *with* the Church, personally present to it "all days, even to the consummation of the age" (Matt 28:20). His is a mission irreducible to a bare moment in history, e.g., to the days when Pontius Pilate was Roman prefect in Israel. Unconfined to the past, vitally operative in the present, it is destined for a climactic future.

It is suitable, then, that the last speech of Jesus be given over to the future, and especially to that part of the future that brings the end of time and the advent of the Reign of God. The speech previews this coming end and warns the Church: Be ready for the end!

THE ESCHATOLOGICAL DISCOURSE (24:1–25:46)

24:1-2	Prediction of the destruction of the temple
24:3-8	Signs of the parousia
24:9-14	Persecutions, betrayals, false prophets
24:15-22	The horrible abomination
24:23-25	Misleading signs and wonders
24:26-31	The coming of the Son of Man
24:32-33	The parable of the fig tree
24:34-36	The time of the parousia
24:37-41	What that day and hour will be like
24:42-44	The example of the householder
24:45-51	The recompense of fidelity/infidelity
25:1-13	The parable of the ten bridesmaids

25:14-30 The parable of the talents
25:31-46 The Last Judgment
        Formula for end of discourse (26:1a)

How is all this material organized? First of all, the introduction to the discourse (24:1-3) has two parts. The first says that the temple will be destroyed. The second is a twofold question placed by the disciples: When will this be, and what will be the sign of Jesus' coming and the close of the age?

There follows the body of the discourse, and it, too, has two parts:

BODY OF DISCOURSE

  I. (24:4-31) Preview of the Coming End
      (A) 24:4-8 The beginning of the sufferings
      (B) 24:9-14 The Tribulation, Part I
      (C) 24:15-28 The Tribulation, Part II
      (D) 24:29-31 Climax (cosmic crack-up), Resolution (Son of Man)

  II. (24:32–25:46) Lesson to Be Drawn: Be Ready for the End!
      (A) 24:32-35 Parable of the fig tree
      (B) 24:36-44 Time of the parousia unknown, so be ready!
      (C) 24:45-51 The recompense of fidelity/infidelity
      (D) 25:1-13 The parable of the ten bridesmaids
      (E) 25:14-30 The parable of the talents
      (F) 25:46 The Last Judgment
      (Formula for end of discourse, 26:1a)

A Note on the Sayings Materials in This Discourse

In the introduction to these five speeches of the Matthean Christ, we said that, by and large, the material came from Jesus, but that its organization in speech form derived from pre-Matthean tradition or from Matthew. The Sermon on the Mount had its sermon character previous to Matthew. Did this sermon character derive from Jesus himself? This is perfectly possible, but on all such matters we can have little critical certainty. The first part of the missionary discourse is a parallel case. It, too, may well have come from Jesus precisely as a short speech, but we cannot establish such matters with great assurance. That Jesus uttered an instruction to his disciples on the future is equally possible.

We have some indications of a relatively small part of the sayings material derived from an early Palestinian community. This held for the ecclesial discourse of Matthew 18, where, for example, there is reference to the practice of fraternal correction (18:15-17) paralleled among the Essenes. Similarly, in the eschatological discourse there is some early Palestinian tradition (reference to special difficulty if it should turn out that the flight from the antichrist should take place on the Sabbath; perhaps a few other images are likewise of post-Easter provenance).

The great mass of material, however, comes from Jesus. Thus there are a fair number of items that, having no parallel in Judaism, derive with solid probability from Jesus himself (some examples: the prophecy of the temple's destruction; the prophecy of martyrdom for his followers; the prophesied fulfillment of Micah's word on coming divisions within Jewish families; the notion that God had already decided to foreshorten the days of distress for the sake of the elect; the several parables that appear in the discourse).

At the same time, we should be aware that the early Church often gave new applications to authentic materials from Jesus. The Jesus of history had had much to say about how pressing the decision of faith/unfaith was, for the Ordeal was about to break out. On the other hand, what he had to say about the very end of time, though qualitatively important, was quantitatively slight. The early Church, awaiting the parousia of the Son of Man and the advent of the Reign of God, drew from the mass of sayings material on the need of decision before it would be too late and transferred it to the Church's expectation of the parousia. (Our interest, to be sure, is not so much in this process as it is in the message that the process has been made to serve.)

INTRODUCTION, Parts I and II

24:1 **Jesus left the temple and was going away, when his disciples**
2 **came and had him look at the buildings of the temple. • But**
he said to them, "You see all these, do you? Truly, I tell you,
there will not be left here one stone upon another; it will all
3 **be torn down." • Then, when he had gone to sit down on the**
Mount of Olives, the disciples came to him privately, saying,
"Tell us, when will this be, and what will be the sign of your
coming and of the close of the age?"

Main Thrust

In the second part of the introduction, the disciples' question is "When? What will be the sign?" But this double question presupposes that there would *be* an end—soon—to temple and time alike. This notion ran flatly counter to ordinary Jewish expectations, which conceived of Jerusalem and the temple as headed not for destruction but for final glorification. Jesus' view, in other words, could not easily be taken for granted. Matthew felt obliged to preface the whole with a positive statement: The temple was doomed! But Matthew presents this prophecy as a simple fact. By the time of the editing of his Gospel, "the doom of the temple" had lost its power to shock Christians. Ever since Jesus' time, the Church had borne the brunt of harsh crackdowns at irregular intervals by the Sadducean temple priesthood.

But Jesus' prophecy of the destruction of the temple did *not* cancel the promises of God respecting Zion, Jerusalem, and

---

24:2: Apropos of Jesus' distinctive view of the temple as doomed, we should not forget that Jesus, from at least the time of Caesarea Philippi, had already transferred to his disciples and followers the biblical affirmation of the inviolability of the holy city, mount, and temple. He had thus already transposed the theme of the inviolability of city and temple to gentile armies to the new sanctuary (built on the rock of Simon) and its inviolability to the assaults of Satan and the powers of death.

the temple, for Jesus had revealed that the true referent of these promises was the Church built on Peter.

I. PREVIEW OF THE COMING END: THE BEGINNING OF THE SUFFERINGS

24:4 **And Jesus answered them, "Take care that no one lead you**
5 **astray. • For many will come in my name, saying, 'I am the**
6 **Christ' and they will lead many astray. • But first you must hear of wars and warnings of war; see that you are not alarmed.**
7 **This indeed must take place, but the end is not yet. • Nation will rise against nation and kingdom against kingdom, and**
8 **in various places there will be famines and earthquakes: • all this is only the beginning of great sufferings."**

Main Thrust

That sufferings would precede the end was a datum of tradition:

> Oh, how mighty is that day,
> there is none like it!
> It is a time of distress for Jacob,
> though there be One who shall yet save him out of it!
> (Jer 30:7)

> There shall be a time of distress such as there never has been
> from when nations began until that time;
> at that time there shall be One to deliver your people,
> everyone whose name is found written in the book.
> (Dan 12:1)

Above, in treating of the missionary discourse, we took note of Jesus' task: to launch the Ordeal. This was not out of love

---

24:5-8: The speech, a religious view of the end of history, draws characteristically on the Scriptures. Citations from biblical tradition and the tradition of Jesus' sayings make up the very substance.

24:5: "Many will come in my name . . . , " i.e., using the name and authority that belong only to me as Christ and Son of God.

24:6: "This indeed must take place" echoes Dan 2:28.

24:7: "Nation will rise against nation" echoes Isa 19:2; 2 Chr 15:6.

of conflict on his part; crisis was indispensable to his winning a response of *faith*. (It would not do merely to have the empty goodwill of spectators.) The task was to gather the remnant of Israel. Only in this remnant would Israel achieve its appointed restoration.

Now, in the fifth and last speech of Jesus, we hear the prophecy that the forces of sin and death will bend every effort to mislead, seduce, and defeat both those called to pledge themselves to Christ and those who had already done so, by confusing them with false claims. Moreover, these forces of mendacity would have an impact!

THE TRIBULATION, Part I

24:9   **"Then people will deliver you up to scourging, and put you to death; and you will be hated by all nations because of my**
10   **name. • And then many will fall, and betray one another,**
11   **and hate one another. • And many false prophets will arise**
12   **and lead many astray. • And owing to the increase of iniq-**
13   **uity, love, on the part of most, will grow cold. • But he who**
14   **endures to the end—there is One who will save him! • And this gospel of the kingdom will be proclaimed throughout the whole world, and promulgated to all peoples; and then the end will come."**

Main Thrust

The disciples had asked: When will the end come? Here they are given a partial answer: Not before the tribulation has

---

24:10: On love growing cold, see the word in Luke 18:8: "When the Son of Man comes, will he find faith on earth?"

24:11: False prophets foreshadow the "abomination" of verse 15.

24:14: This belonged to the common heritage of early Christian missionary theology; only when the "full number" of gentiles destined to be saved was reached would the end come, and with it the salvation of all Israel. (Also worth noting: The present text, which reflects an experience of the Christian mission in the Mediterranean, differs markedly from Matt 10:23, which envisaged the end of the world coming while the disciples were still limited to Israel.)

wreaked its havoc (persecution of Christians; martyrdom; apostasy of many; betrayal and mutual hatred; false prophecy; the loss of fervent love). In the face of these future phenomena, Jesus calls for a courageous determination to hold out to the end. Second, the end will not come before the news of salvation proclaimed by Jesus and rehearsed in the present work of Matthew will be heard by the whole world.

THE TRIBULATION, Part II

24:15 "So when you see the horrible abomination spoken of by the prophet Daniel, standing in the holy place (let the reader [of
16 holy Writ] understand), • then let those who are in Judea flee
17 to the mountains; • let whoever is on the housetop-terrace
18 not go down to take what is in his house; • and let whoever
19 is in the field not turn back for his cloak. • And alas for those who are with child and those who give suck in those days!
20 Pray that your flight may not be in winter or on a Sabbath.
21   "Then there will be a calamity greater than there has ever been from the beginning of the world until now, and than

---

24:15: In older English translations of Dan 12:11 (cf. 9:27), we meet the expression "the abomination of desolation," rendered more exactly "the abominable thing causing desolation." This referred originally to the Syrian king Antiochus Epiphanes, who in 168 B.C. desecrated the altar of the temple. But in accord with the tendency to reinterpret such charged texts as prophecies still to be fulfilled, the phrase came to be thought of as still looking for its true referent. Possibly our text is a Jewish Christian composition from the period when the Emperor Gaius Caligula (according to *Josephus and *Philo) was threatening to set up a statue of himself in the temple. But the Matthean redactor (or "Greek Matthew") no doubt understood the phrase to refer to a still future event: the appearance of "the man of lawlessness, the son of perdition" (2 Thess 2:3), or "antichrist" (1 John 2:18; 4:3).

24:20: This word doubtless reflects a community of Palestinian Jewish Christians who committed themselves to strict Torah observance. The Torah forbade traveling farther than just over half a mile on the Sabbath.

24:21: See *Ordeal.

22   there ever will be. • And if those days had not been shortened, no living being would be saved; but for the sake of
23   the elect the time will be cut short. • Then if anyone says to
you, 'Lo, here is the Christ!' or 'There he is!' do not believe it.
24   For false Christs and false prophets will arise and show great
signs and wonders, so as to lead astray, if possible, even the
25-26 elect. • Lo, I have told you beforehand. • So, if they say to
you, 'Lo, he is in the wilderness,' do not go out; if they say,
27   'Lo, he is in the inner rooms,' do not believe it. • For as the
lightning from the east flashes as far as the west, so will be
28   the coming of the Son of Man. • Wherever the body is, there
the eagles will be gathered together.''

Main Thrust

Here is what will happen en route to the end: first, there
will be "the horrible abomination" predicted by Daniel (Dan
9:27; 12:11), that is, the appearance of "the man of lawlessness, the son of perdition" (2 Thess 2:3), or "the antichrist"
(1 John 2:18; 4:3). When he appears, it is time for flight. Second, the great tribulation (Dan 12:1; see Joel 2:2) will take place,
with rumors, false christs and prophets (in support of the great
denier, the antichrist). Third, suddenly the Son of Man will
come.

CLIMAX (Cosmic Crack-up), RESOLUTION (Son of Man)

24:29 ''Immediately after the calamity of those days the sun will
grow dark, and the moon will cease to give its light, and the
stars will fall from heaven, and the powers of the heavens

24:22: The standard Jewish view was that God's plans for the
world were inalterable (e.g., 4 Ezra 4:37). Jesus, by contrast, assumes
God's ability to change his mind.

24:28: The proverb (akin to "Where there's smoke, there's fire")
said: "Wherever the corpse is, there the vultures will be gathered together." Matthew might just possibly have said "eagles" to allude
to the Romans, who had eagles on their standards.

30 will be shaken; • then will appear the sign of the Son of Man
in heaven, and then all the tribes of the earth will mourn,
and they will see the Son of Man coming on the clouds of
31 heaven with great power and glory; • and he will send out
his angels with a loud trumpet call, and they will gather his
elect from the four winds, from one end of heaven to the
other."

Main Thrust

This passage concludes the preview of the end: The tribulation is followed by the crack-up of the cosmos and the appearance of the Son of Man. The crack-up is epitomized by
sun, moon, stars, and the firmament: the sun and the moon
grow dark; one after another the stars fall from the sky; the
firmament (the sky under the image of an inverted bowl) is
shaken as by an earthquake. The resolution is the sudden appearance of the "sign" or banner of the Son of Man, to which
the dispersed people of Christ can rally. This is the definitive
bad news for the scoffers and the powers of sin and death,
who plunge into mourning; it is definitive good news for the
chosen, the faithful, whom the angels gather up, following
their trumpet call.

II. LESSON: BE READY FOR THE END.
PARABLE OF THE FIG TREE

24:32 "From the fig tree learn this comparison: as soon as its
branches grow tender and put forth their leaves, you know
33 that summer is near. • So also, when you see all these things,
34 you know that he is near, at the very gates. • Truly, I say to
you, this generation shall not pass away till all these things
35 take place. • Heaven and earth will pass away, but my words
will not pass away."

24:32: Originally the parable of the fig tree was meant to evoke
God's promise of salvation. Here it is applied to dark signs and
portents.

Main Thrust

When the fig tree loses its leaves, its appearance is distinctive among the trees of Palestine: the bare, spiky twigs give it the appearance of being utterly dead. As the sap rises and its shoots burst with life, the fig tree becomes a natural symbol of the mystery of life out of death. Its promise of summer yields the lesson: Christ is near!

TIME OF THE PAROUSIA UNKNOWN, SO BE READY!

24:36   "But of [when] that day and hour [will come] no one knows a thing,
          not even the angels of heaven,
          nor the Son, but the Father alone.

37   As it was in the days of Noah
      so shall it be at the coming of the Son of Man:

38   For as in those days before the flood
          they were eating and drinking,
          marrying and giving in marriage,
          until the day when Noah entered the ark

39   and they knew nothing
      till the flood came and swept them all away.
      So will be the coming of the Son of Man.

40   Then two men will be in the field;
      one is taken and one is left.

41   Two women will be grinding at the mill;
      one is taken and one is left.

24:36: Since the historical Jesus did not refer to himself as "the Son," it is doubtful whether this saying is historical. In any case, while placing Jesus higher than the angels, it does not deal with divine knowledge but only with human, prophetic knowledge.

24:37-39: Jesus' image of the days of Noah and the sudden Deluge were originally applied to the sudden coming of the Ordeal. It was a warning against Israel's unresponsiveness to the looming end. Oral tradition reformulated "the days of Noah," converting the image into a warning to await alertly the advent of the Son of Man.

24:40-41: "Taken": taken into the Reign of God; "left": left for destruction.

42 Watch, then, for you do not know on what day your Lord is
43 coming. • But know this: If the householder knew in what
   part of the night the thief was coming, he would keep watch
44 and would not let his house be broken into. • Therefore you
   also must be ready; for the Son of Man is coming at an hour
   you do not expect."

Main Thrust

As indicated earlier (p. 92), Jesus' scenario of the future was
prophetic and symbolic; instructed in accord with it, the disciples, like John the Baptist before Jesus and like the Apostle
Paul after him, expected an early consummation of time and
history. When this failed to take place, the followers of Jesus
gradually adjusted to the actuality of history, just as ancient
Israel had always done, not by finding a satisfactory intellectual solution, but by muddling through with persevering faith.
The lesson dominating the second part of the eschatological
discourse is readiness for the end, whenever it comes.

This begins with the word on the Father's knowledge of
the day and the hour. Since the Gospel of Matthew deals with
the Son's human, prophetic knowledge and not with his divine knowledge, we see why it is said that knowledge of the
end is reserved to the Father.

The Christian response to not knowing the day and the hour
is not to drop the whole matter of the future consummation;
it is rather to adopt an attitude of alert watchfulness. The parable of the thief at night (Matt 24:43-44) has been made a parable of the parousia, its lesson being precisely one of alert
watchfulness.

24:43: What is said of the Noah image can be said of the parable
of the thief at night. Originally the parable had an altogether sim-
pler, non-allegorical character and functioned as a warning to be ready
for the sudden outbreak of the Ordeal.

THE RECOMPENSE OF FIDELITY/INFIDELITY

24:45   "If then there be a faithful and wise servant set by his mas-
        ter over his household to give them their food at the proper
46   time, • happy indeed will that servant be whom his master,
47   when he comes, shall find so doing. • Truly, I tell you, he
48   will set him over all his goods. • But if he is a wicked ser-
49   vant, and says to himself, 'My master is delayed,' • and
        begins to beat his fellow servants, and eats and drinks with
50   the drunken, • the master of that servant will come on a day
        when he does not expect him and at an hour he does not
51   know, • and will cut him off, and assign him a lot with the
        hypocrites; there men will weep and gnash their teeth."

Main Thrust

The parable clearly deals with the parousia of the Lord, its
delay, and the judgment of Church leaders when it comes. It
features a particular facet of the "Be ready!" theme. In this
ecclesial Gospel, Church leaders above all must show themselves faithful fulfillers of the Lord's will. What is at stake? Not
just status, but eternal destiny, never to be taken for granted.

THE PARABLE OF THE TEN BRIDESMAIDS

25:1   "Then the Reign of heaven shall be like ten maidens who
2   took their lamps and went to meet the bridegroom. • Five of
3   them were foolish and five were wise. • For when the fool-

---

24:45-51: The parable of the servant entrusted with supervision,
here a parousia parable, was originally a warning to the scribes, national religious leaders, that they were about to be called to account.
Verse 51 is a Matthean touch.

25:1-13: The parable of the ten bridesmaids, like so much of the
material in this discourse, changes the audience from Jesus' critics
to his followers, and the theme from warning of the Ordeal to the
theme of being watchful for the parousia.

The concluding exhortation to watchfulness fits the parable's reference to the parousia but does not fit its imagery: all the maidens slept,
not just the foolish ones. The error, according to the parable itself,
was the failure to bring oil for the lamps. Originally this probably re-

4 ish took their lamps, they took no oil with them; • but the
5 wise took oil in flasks together with their lamps. • As the
   bridegroom was delayed, they all grew drowsy and fell
6 asleep. • But halfway through the night there was a cry, 'Be-
7 hold, the bridegroom! Come out to meet him.' • Then all those
8 maidens arose and trimmed their lamps. • And the foolish
   said to the wise, 'Give us some of your oil, for our lamps are
9 going out.' • But the wise replied, 'There may not be enough
   for us and you; go rather to the dealers and buy for your-
10 selves.' • And while they went to buy, the bridegroom came,
   and those who were ready went in with him to the marriage
11 feast; and the door was shut. • Afterward, the other maidens
12 came also, saying, 'Lord, lord, open to us.' • But he replied,
13 'Truly, I tell you, I do not know you.' • Watch, therefore,
   for you know neither the day nor the hour.''

Main Thrust

Originally simple, the parable has been allegorized: The ten
bridesmaids are the Christian community; the bridegroom is
the parousiac Christ; the delay of the bridegroom is the delay
of the parousia; his sudden coming is the unexpected advent
of the parousia; the rejection of the foolish maidens is condemnation at the Last Judgment. Lesson: Judgment comes before
the banquet of salvation! Get ready for it! (This theme seals
the vision of the Gospel as central to God's plan for all time
and the whole world.)

THE PARABLE OF THE TALENTS

25:14 ''For it is like a man going on a journey who called his ser-
   15 vants and entrusted to them his property. • To one he gave
       five talents, to another two, to another one, to each accord-

---

ferred to the wisdom of persevering faith as the response to Jesus'
preaching.
   25:14-30: Adaptation of the parable from ''crisis parable'' envisag-
ing the coming Ordeal to ''parousia parable'' on watchfulness for the
return of Jesus accounts for some details that were not original: the

16 ing to his ability. Then he went away. • He who had received the five talents went at once to make the most of them; and

17 he made five talents more. • So also he who had the two tal-

18 ents gained two talents more. • But he who had received the one talent went and dug a hole in the ground and hid his

19 master's money. • Now after a long time the master of those

20 servants came and settled accounts with them. • And he who had received the five talents came forward, bringing five talents more, saying, 'Master, you turned five talents over to

21 me; here are five talents more that I gained.' • His master said to him, 'Well done, good and faithful servant; you have been faithful over less, I will set you over more. Enter into

22 the banquet of your master.' • And he also who had the two talents came forward, saying, 'Master, you turned two tal-

23 ents over to me; here are two more that I gained.' • His master said to him, 'Well done, good and faithful servant; you have been faithful over less, I will set you over more. Enter

24 into the banquet of your master.' • He who had received the one talent also came forward, saying, 'Master, I knew you to be a hard man, set on reaping where you did not sow and

25 gathering where you did not winnow; • so I was afraid, and I went and hid your talent in the ground. Here is what is

26 yours.' • But his master answered him, 'You wicked and slothful servant! You knew that I like to reap where I did not

27 sow, and to gather where I did not winnow? • Then you ought to have invested my money with the bankers, and at my coming I should have received what was mine with interest.

28 So take the talent from him, and give it to him who has ten.

29 For to everyone who has will more be given, and he will have abundance; but from him who has not, even what he has will

30 be taken away. • And cast the worthless servant into the outer darkness; there men will weep and gnash their teeth.' "

---

addressing of the parable to disciples rather than critics, e.g., the scribes; the extravagantly high amounts of money; the application to the parable of the proverb in verse 29 (on how the rich get richer, and the poor get poorer); "outer darkness," etc.

Main Thrust

Both the placement of this parable and the concluding reference to "outer darkness," weeping, and gnashing of teeth show that Matthew refers the parable to parousia and judgment. As for the concrete sense of judgment here, the lesson is: Unproductive non-transgression is not enough. Perhaps with Church leaders above all in mind, the message is: "From each according to his or her ability."

THE LAST JUDGMENT

25:31   "Now, when the Son of Man comes in his glory, and all the
32   angels with him, then he will sit on his glorious throne • and
    all the nations will be assembled before him; and he will separate them all, one from another, as a shepherd separates the
33   sheep from the goats; • and he will place the sheep on his
34   right hand and the goats on his left. • Then the King will say to those on his right, 'Come, O blessed of my Father, inherit the Kingdom prepared for you from the foundation of
35   the world; • for I was hungry and you gave me food, I was thirsty and you gave me drink, I was a stranger and you wel-
36   comed me, • I was naked and you clothed me, I was sick and you visited me, I was in prison and you came to see me.'
37   Then the righteous will answer him, 'Lord, when did we see thee hungry and feed thee, or thirsty and give thee drink?
38   And when did we see thee a stranger and welcome thee, or
39   naked and clothe thee? • And when did we see thee sick or

---

25:31, 34: Note the correlation between "Son of Man" and "King." Clearly, both are messianic. (Whether this was already essentially true of Jesus' own usage or arose after him in the course of oral tradition is disputed.)

25:32: At night the Palestinian shepherd would separate the sheep and the goats of his mixed flock to make provision for keeping the goats warm.

25:33: The sheep are the more valuable of the two kinds of animals. Being white, they were a more appropriate image for the righteous than the black goats were.

40 in prison and visit thee?' • And the King will answer them,
     'Truly, I tell you, whatever you did to any of the least of these
41 my brethren, you did to me.' • Then he will say to those at
     his left, 'Depart from me you cursed, into the eternal fire pre-
42 pared for the devil and his angels; • for I was hungry and
     you gave me no food, I was thirsty and you gave me no drink,
43 I was a stranger and you did not welcome me, naked and you
     did not clothe me, sick and in prison and you did not visit
44 me.' • Then they also will answer, 'Lord, when did we see
     thee hungry or thirsty or a stranger or naked or sick or in
45 prison, and did not minister to thee?' • Then he will answer
     them, 'Truly, I tell you, whatever you did not do to any of
46 the least of these, you did not do to me.' • And they will go
     away into eternal punishment, but the righteous into eternal
     life.''

Main Thrust

First, the scene that is conjured up is that of the Last Judgment, a theme that reached its true and full proportions with
the rise of apocalyptic literature and the notion of human existence ongoing beyond this life. The question that the scene
is designed to answer is: What is the criterion of good and evil
in the sight of God? (Or, more concretely: We know how we
are to be judged, namely, in accord with the Torah; but the
gentiles, who have no Torah, how are they to be judged?) The
answer is: On the basis of practical compassion (known in Judaism as ''works of love'') for the poor, the miserable, the down
and out.

It is noteworthy that the compassionate among the nations
are completely surprised at the words of the King. They are
altogether unconscious of ever having seen, known, and
served him. They know nothing of the Jewish tradition (e.g.,
Mid. Tan 15, 9) according to which God says to Israel, ''My
children, when you gave food to the poor, I counted it as
though you had given it to me.'' They know nothing of the
conception of the Messiah hidden in the persons of the poor
and the wretched (e.g., Mark 9:37 = Luke 9:48; cf. Matt 18:5:

"Whoever receives one such child in my name receives me; and whoever receives me receives not me but him who sent me.")

The Sense of the Eschatological Discourse as a Whole

How the world ends throws a powerful light on the whole of its past, showing what finally counts. Divine revelation specifies the main field of meaning. This is, above all, the God of Israel's sending of his Son.

For Israel, authentic value is mediated by God's word through his servants; for the nations it is mediated by encounter with the helpless. These two sets of values mesh. The word of God in the tradition of Israel demanded mercy for the helpless; for the gentiles, unbeknownst to them, history has been an encounter with the grace of God in Christ, reconciling the world to himself.

The present scheme of things in its entirety is indeed coming to an end. In fact, the temple will be among the first things to be destroyed. All the meaningless motion and futile chit-chat of the world will soon be gone, yielding to the supreme issues of faith and unfaith, good and evil.

The Ordeal foreshadowing the end will be calamitous. The power of evil, of lies, death, and destruction, of Satan and his tool, the antichrist, will be so overwhelming that if God had not already decided for the sake of the elect to abbreviate those days, no one would escape their ravages.

The world will pass, the sun and moon will grow dark, the stars will fall out of the sky. But the Son of Man will come as promised, accompanied by his angels. Pray, then, not to fall victim to the affliction, or Ordeal. And do not give up on the coming of the Son of Man. Be faithful servants. Let your service accord with the favoritism of God and of the Son of Man for the downtrodden and poor, the simple, the afflicted, the outcast.

Chapter 7

APPROPRIATE RESPONSE TO
THE FIVE SPEECHES TODAY

By way of completing consideration of these five speeches, which, owing to the Christian liturgy, have been the most powerful and influential in history, we shift the focus from the speeches to their audience, i.e., to us listeners and readers. What kind of response should we bring to them? This has never been an easy question, and never an insignificant one. It has long been a conscious question, however, beginning with Jesus himself. We said above, in regard to Matthew's avoidance of the word "teach" to describe Jesus' addressing parables to the crowd (see above, p. 78), that there is no teaching where there is no learning. Now we add: There is no learning when the response to the teacher is inappropriate. For all five speeches today: Jesus offers authentic prophetic teaching only on condition that the listener or reader responds *appropriately* to him.

Speaker and Speeches Define Appropriate Response

If we look into Jesus' mission as a study in communications, we find a clear-cut, consistent communications strategy. The following three are among its salient traits: a mix of verbal and non-verbal expression (*symbolic action); an avoidance of stately, grandiose language and, correspondingly, a marked preference for concrete, everyday language; an avoidance of claims and titles and, correspondingly, a strong and consistent preference for the forms and techniques of indirection (e.g., the parable form).

These traits serve and attest a controlling aspect of Jesus' mission: crystal clarity on the kind of response he wished to elicit, insight into how to elicit that kind of response, and rock-firm determination to elicit nothing less than that kind of response. The response in question was, of course, *faith*. Jesus wanted his listeners to discover on their own what the uniquely appropriate response to him and to his words was, and, secondly, to place the self-committing act of that response.

Of all the responses the most common, and the least appropriate, was *spectator opinion*. Jesus did his utmost to jar his listeners out of this bland, uncommitted superficiality. Analysis of his parables time and again reveals an intense effort of this sort. A good part of Jesus' insistent warning to the crowds that time was short and the Ordeal imminent was meant to subvert trivial responses.

The intention of the speaker and the nature of the speeches determine what responses are appropriate. Whether sympathetic or unsympathetic, the non-committal reaction of the mere spectator falls woefully short. It did in the days of Jesus, and it does today as well. The depiction of crowd responses in the Synoptic Gospels is mostly limited to a *stereotypic feature of the form "miracle story." But these three Gospels do add indirect evidence of the crowds' reactions by presenting Jesus' own reactions—sometimes vigorous, sometimes poignant—to the indifference or hostility of listeners or onlookers: rebukes, reproaches, warnings, expressions of anger (Mark 1:43), amazement (Mark 6:6), sorrow (Mark 3:5), savagely bitter humor (Luke 13:33).

The Fourth Gospel offers a complex picture. Spectator opinion occasionally turns into controversy; under such pressure some find themselves pushed into opposition (John 7:15-20), while others are led toward faith (John 7:25-31). Often, of course, opinion remains just that—shallow and wavering (e.g., John 7:35-36, 40-43, 46, 51; 10:20-21, but see 10:40-42).

We have been engaged in acknowledging that "speaker" and "speeches" have a role in defining the listener's appropriate response. But, thus far without particular emphasis, we have all along understood "the speaker" as not only Jesus but the Matthean Jesus, the Jesus whom Matthew has set before us to address us, the Matthean readership. Before going on to further considerations, we might pause here to add that the Gospel of Matthew as "a verbal contraption" and distinctive "vision of the good" has a role in defining an appropriate response to the five speeches today. Intelligent readers take account of context. Here the first claim to "context" respecting the speeches accrues to the Gospel of Matthew.

Modern Philosophy of Religion
Throws Light on Appropriate Response

That Jesus was intensely set on winning a faith-response and, given the nature of his initiatives, spectator opinion fell far short of the appropriate response is unambiguous in the Gospel literature. Furthermore, since the mid-nineteenth century, when mere opinion seemed to many a reasonable alternative to "faith" and "dogmas," there has grown up a tradition of protest in favor of classical Christianity. Søren *Kierkegaard protested in 1844 against *Hegelian substitutes for faith, and, partly under his delayed influence, Christian theology in the twentieth century took up "faith" as the sole appropriate response whether to the message of Jesus or to the *kerygma of the Church. "How interesting!" is an inept, failed response to a life-and-death message.

Kierkegaard's protest took the form of a philosophical essay contrasting Socrates and Jesus, philosophy and faith.[7] The contrast between the two is most graphic and intense when "history" comes into the picture. To Socrates—the symbol, for Kierkegaard, of all philosophy—history was neither a source nor a ground of truth. Perhaps, like other Greek thinkers, he understood time to be a cycle without beginning or end. History established nothing. If, however, by "a project of thought" one were to posit a divine teacher who, in the form of "servant," entered time from eternity to lead the human subject to discover something utterly new, without which he had hitherto been in error; if, further, one were to posit that the human subject was now given not only the truth but the power to affirm it as such, would it not follow that a certain moment in history had made a difference? Would not this moment be well named "the fullness of time"?

In this "project of thought" the writer (Kierkegaard used a pseudonym, "Johannes Climacus," and allowed his own name to stand merely as "responsible for publication") was careful to emphasize that the power to affirm the truth was and is every bit as much a divine gift as the truth itself. This power was and is "faith"; and in the perspective offered by Johannes Climacus, faith was as necessary to one who was contemporary with "the teacher" as it was for someone of the next generation or of the third or fourth or fiftieth generation later than "the teacher." All would equally stand in need of faith. A moment in history would thus become the key to truth and salvation. To the teacher, to his word, to the fullness of time, the uniquely appropriate response was *faith*. The one thing necessary was that faith be divinely given.

Kierkegaard's "project of thought" has a distinct subtlety and personal contour, but for our purposes there is no need to enter into the details and nuances of his thought. His central point is clear and easily comprehensible. Despite the Socratic view that history does not count, an entirely different view is possible. History counts enormously, incalculably, *if at a moment in time God entered history to alter it permanently from within.* And all the complexities of European thought on history and on the limits of historical knowledge from the seventeenth to the nineteenth century are relativized by a single insight: The most crucial aspect of the human response to the key moment of history is *the gift of faith.* And just as God, according to this "project of thought," gives us this servant, savior, and teacher, so God regularly and generously gives—he does not withhold—the capacity to affirm the truth of the teacher's words.

Our answer, then, to the practical question of what kind of response to these five speeches is appropriate is: the response of faith or unfaith. The refusal of faith is a more appropriate response to these speeches than a spectator's non-committal admiration, for it acknowledges, if only negatively and inadequately, the speeches' deadly serious level of appeal. But to respond both appropriately *and* adequately is, by God's grace, to place the self-committing act of faith.

Childish Faith Not a Wholly Adequate Response

It is nonetheless true that a fully positive, satisfactory response to the five speeches today is not entirely settled by these reflections of Johannes Climacus/Søren Kierkegaard. We should frankly confess that Kierkegaard's great contribution was incomplete. It is important, yet not enough, to settle the matter of ''faith and history'' from the standpoint of faith. As adult believers, we must also confront the challenge of living on the level of our own times with respect to history. It will not do to take refuge in a faith that slips easily from childlike to childish, recoiling from problems and complexities and so missing out on available solutions and occasional insights and illuminations.

Gospel criticism and historical-Jesus research from the 1840s to World War I (especially in Germany, where such study was most intensely cultivated) too frequently had the simplemindedness to present itself and its conclusions as *an alternative to faith*. Bit by bit, however, it has become clear that a truly authentic role for this research is quite different. Historical knowledge is not a substitute for, not an alternative to, faith. On the other hand, it *can* function in a positive way, namely, as a resource relevant to faith and in the service of faith. What can history do for faith?

Faith is faith, whether it be the faith of a simple child or of a sophisticated adult. It is an infused virtue, a power that no human being or consideration or good intention can bring into being. It is a gift of God. ''No one can come to me unless the Father, who sent me, draw him'' (John 6:44). Historical knowledge does not add to or detract from the integrity of faith. It may nevertheless impinge on faith, informing it, allowing it to be more intelligent, more reasonable, more responsible. Such service is limited and is not to be exaggerated; still, it is far from valueless. It provides us with the possibility of putting aside an unbecoming naiveté in matters of faith and adopting a suitably adult hold on our most precious religious heritage.

The rise of the historical consciousness has helped us to recognize this aspect of faith relative to philosophy, history, science, and knowledge in general. One great forward step beyond the schools of thought (such as *the School of Alexandria) that grew up in Christian antiquity lay in the modern acknowledgment that there are biblical texts which we have not understood, do not understand, and in all probability will never understand. When the School of Alexandria and its many heirs in antiquity, the Middle Ages, the Renaissance and post-Renaissance eras met difficulties in the understanding of biblical texts, they invariably solved them. Looking back on these solutions from the historical consciousness of the present, we may be pardoned for finding in them a certain naive self-deception. The solutions were artificial, a mix of knowledge and mystification. The historical consciousness has freed us from our illusory ambitions of complete understanding. The modern interpreter does not find it necessary, nor even very comfortable, to pretend to understand everything. The community of modern interpreters is intent on progress toward a fuller understanding, with the sober but cheering reflection that if one's own generation fails to solve a particular set of problems, the next generation may do better. Meanwhile, no one is encouraged to make futile claims to comprehensive understanding.

How many verses in the five speeches remain more or less opaque? A fair number. Since we understand "the parts" only to the extent that we understand "the whole" and vice versa, it follows that all five speeches remain to some extent opaque to all of us. (It is most instructive to discover what fine interpreters from other epochs made of these same texts and how much we have both gained and lost. But even with patristic and medieval help, our grasp of these five speeches remains imperfect.)

What Is an Appropriate Response Today?

To speak of the meaning of the five speeches in Matthew *today* might give the false impression that we today are authorized to assign them a meaning different from the meaning they have always had. Their meaning, however (and here, of course, we allude to *intended meaning*), is essentially fixed. The issue of "today" bears on how we might bring that meaning to bear on *the needs of today*. Every age, though it shares needs with every other age, also has quite distinctive needs of its own. How can we call on these speeches to meet these needs?

In each generation since the Christian liturgy focused on Matthew as the master catechist of the apostolic age, the speeches have made their way into a changing world to change it in the image of Christ. They did so by meeting both the common needs and the special needs of each generation. So the effort to define what the five speeches mean today turns on how one construes and evaluates our own specific needs as well as the needs we have in common with others.

We might begin by calling to mind the latter: our common religious needs, the ones we share with all generations, and in particular with the readers and hearers of these speeches across two millennia. These needs are neither as obvious nor compelling as material needs of food and shelter; the need and good of order, which is met by the family and other social structures; the need of civil society, which is met by political organization. Needs of a religious kind are more akin to cultural needs, and cultural needs are met by the cultivation of values. Not on bread alone doth man live. Still, religious needs are neither identical with nor reducible to cultural needs, for they bear not only on meaning and value but on ultimate meaning and value.

We might get along without religion if only we could get along without ultimate meaning. But we cannot, for we cannot persevere in living intelligently, reasonably, and responsibly without some hold on ultimate context. "To live intelligently, reasonably, responsibly, an adult has to form some view of the universe," Bernard Lonergan observed. Moreover, he added, the same adult must form some idea of his place and role in the universe along with his fellow human beings:

> He may do so by appealing to myth, or to science, or to philosophy, or to religion. . . . A mythic solution will do only for the immature. A scientific solution is impossible, for science methodically and systematically refuses to consider the issue. A philosophic solution is out-of-date, for philosophy has become existential; it is concerned with man in his concrete existing; and there the issue is authenticity.[8]

But, argued Lonergan, the human subject exists *authentically* in the measure that he or she succeeds in *self-transcendence, which has its fulfillment and its ground in God's gift of his love to us. In short, religion is a critical and, when all is said and done, an indispensable resource for integral human authenticity.

Another way of making the same point is to note how the need for religion is bound up with the need for personal fulfillment. Religion, to be sure, teaches the love of God for his own sake. But this, so far from keeping religion from playing a key role in the drive to human fulfillment, is the paradoxical secret of this fulfillment. Self-realization is the fruit of self-transcendence, just as surely as self-destructiveness is the fruit of egotism, or self-centeredness.

The five speeches in Matthew's Gospel have always served this set of basic human needs. A view of the universe, of our place in the universe and of our role along with others in it, is just what these speeches provide. They specify a way, indeed a divinely revealed way, of responding wisely and generously to the love of God and the situation of the human being in the world. They teach us not to close off our minds and hearts from the initiative of God toward us, and, more positively, they teach us how to make a grateful love of God take root in our life. By offering unique and powerful guidance to self-transcendence, they open a way to basic human fulfillment. For our fulfillment lies in significant part in the development, the coming to full flower, of our potential and in the capacity to recognize the good and to take joy in it.

The speeches, while supposing the gift of God to us in his Son, highlight the Son's own way of receiving and responding to this gift. It is the Son who makes possible the ideal of virtue (the bringing of human potential to its uttermost fulfillment) and love (the capacity of taking joy in the good). He establishes a cause worth serving, a common life worth living, a past worth remembering, and a future worth hoping for.

Such is the sense of aspiring to be, like him and with him, a light to our surrounding world, of returning good for evil, of abandoning the entanglements of anxiety, of concentrating our suspicions and corrections not on others but on ourselves. Such is the sense of steeling ourselves for the crises that otherwise might overwhelm us, of giving our best effort to making life livable in our surrounding world and in the communion of the Church. Such is the sense of expanding our horizons beyond the limits of this world and this life to include the new creation begun by the life of faith and to be consummated in God's Reign.

What about the possible special meanings of the five speeches for the world and generation of today? We said above that any answer will hinge on how we construe and evaluate our own distinctive situation in the world. This is not the rational world of the Enlightenment, not the nineteenth-century world that reinterpreted Christianity as a riddle, burden, and purely private affair, abandoning it to plunge into commerce and imperial ambition. No, our century is different, and yet it is the product of the previous two.

First, it has not only witnessed the ruthless conflict of ideologies, but it remains an age of ongoing ideological struggle.

The racist ideology of Nazi Germany met its end in the 1940s, but this did not cure the world of racism. The most murderous ideology in history, that of Soviet Communism, has been recently buried with minimal lament, but the same ideology survives, crippled, in China and elsewhere, including Western academic and other elites. Meanwhile, nineteenth-century liberal philosophy in its contemporary heirs has lost much of the vision and generosity that attended its rise, replacing them with a sour, envious form of egalitarianism and blindness to simple but basic human values—all traits of anti-religious ideology. Finally, the humane regard for and cultivation of freedom can become a ruthless drive to create a culture that consciously repudiates all limits as alienating.

What do the five great speeches contribute to the struggle against ideology? First, "ideology," ever since the origin of the term in the French Revolution and era of Napoleon, but even more markedly since its use by Karl Marx, is a rationalization of some alienation. It is a good thing to dismantle a rationalization; it is even better, more basic and more effective, to dissipate the alienation being rationalized. But what more potent antidote is there to alienation than the love of God and the love of neighbor?

We should avoid simplicities, however, and the illusions that easily infect and undermine the pure desire for truth. It is not enough to invoke "love." We must attempt to deal concretely, even if briefly, with particular traits of contemporary alienation and ideology, and with particular meanings and values highlighted in the five speeches.

Depersonalization leading to a sense of powerlessness and estrangement—such is the alienation that is not defeated, not dissipated, but merely rationalized by ideology. Can such traits as powerlessness and estrangement survive the sense of being deeply and personally loved by God, the Omnipotent, and by Christ, the Savior he sent into the world and raised from the dead? An individual person conscious that Christ "loved me and handed himself over [to death] for me" (Gal 2:20), a group persuaded that he "freed us from our sins by his blood'' because ''he loves us'' (Rev 1:5), a worldwide community understanding itself as ''one new man, in place of two'' (Eph 2:15; cf. 4:24), that is, as a new humanity of Jew and gentile, intensely aware that ''Christ loved us and gave himself up [to death] for us'' (Eph 5:2), are all, we can predict, enviably free of alienation.

The ''essential Christian experience'' can be defined variously, but we may focus for a moment on a constant in all the definitions, namely, a powerful conviction that Christ, ''having loved his own who were in the world, loved them to the end'' (John 13:1). It is the Christian awareness that before we gave him so much as a passing thought, Christ died for us. As Paul put it, ''While we were helpless, at the right time, Christ died for the ungodly'' (Rom 5:6), and ''while we were yet sinners, Christ died for us'' (Rom 5:8). One aspect of the alienations that ravage our time, deftly camouflaged by ideology, is the now glib, now tacit denial of sin, and the evacuation of meaning from guilt. By contrast, at the base of the above convictions is the confession of sin and the acknowledgment of guilt. A top-drawer ideologist of the nineteenth and twentieth centuries, Lenin, insisted on the basic role of hatred in his solution; knowing whereof he spoke, he was entirely right. Love has an equally basic role in its reversal.

A most prominent feature of contemporary ideology in Western societies, be it Marxist or post-Liberal, is the odd mixture of, on the one hand, insistence on ''realism'' and ''demystification'' and, on the other, an extravagant *utopianism. Latent contradiction is the hallmark of ideology. These ideological contradictions are not merely theoretical. They tend, rather, to be murderous. Marxists in Russia and China, with their burning passion for a better world, liquidated an estimated hundred million enemies of the people. The ideal of a pure Germany and a pure Europe was public, but what it meant was, as long as possible, kept secret: the killing of Jews, Slavs, Gypsies, and other racial and religious ''trash.'' ''Marching for women'' in celebration of the legal right to kill unborn children, half of them girls, has ''ideology'' written all over it.

Out of the five speeches in Matthew's Gospel we may derive elements of a view of "the human dilemma" and of its solution. Insofar as "the solution" affirms an end to history, a judgment of the world, and a victorious Reign of God, it, too, is extravagantly utopian. But we might give a moment's thought to the difference between the utter irrealism of this-worldly solutions among ideologies of all stripes and the utter realism of the Matthean solution so far as this world is concerned.

In the view of Matthew's Gospel, the mission of Christ is already enough of a confirmed success to guarantee total success in the post-historical "age to come." But so far as this life is concerned, the pattern is akin to that of Christ himself in this life. It is a struggle to bring under control anger and lust and whatever sour joy there is in being a blusterer, an avenger, a good hater (Matt 5:21-22, 27-30, 33-36, 38-39, 43-45). Piety is right; but since prestige is dangerous, if not fatal, to it, piety is to be purged by the demand that it be *secret* (6:1-6, 16-18).

As long as this life lasts, "the solution" will call for courage, even heroic courage, made possible by the gift of God (Matt 10:17-39). There is no irrealism here, no positing of a new, imaginary species of humanity. If, as we remarked apropos of the parables, "we are called to be saints," this is precisely in the realist context of an ongoing struggle. And the sheer joy of the disciple—he has found the "treasure hidden in a field" and the "one pearl of great price" (13:44-46)—shines out of a backdrop of darkness. This holds true, too, for the life of the Church (18:1-35), which, for all its miseries and failures (13:24-30, 36-43, 47-50), is a fellowship of forgiveness (18:15-35).

We should be neither impressed nor upset if the ideologists of our time ridicule the "utopianism" of faith for its positing of a coming judgment of the world and a post-historical Reign of God. For one thing, the pendulum has swung. Many ideologies have lost ground. Even as new ideologies arise, the ideologists' hold on *cosmopolis (the international community of those concerned with meanings and values) has lately weakened. Whatever unbelievers might think of the world judgment and the Reign of God, the life of faith has gained ground in the public forum.

We all know in our bones that in faith there is some strange and secret bond with the real. Faith has proven to have lasting-power, which of itself has set faith apart from and superior to the ideologies of our time. It is clear, moreover, that some of them, at least, have already taken so dreadful a toll that they have been all but universally repudiated as murderous illusions. Who can number their victims or justify the pile of corpses reaching into the sky? By comparison, Christianity, however puzzling in its affirmations, seems sane, realistic, and benevolent.

Conclusion

The appropriate response to the five speeches is to let them continue to change the world. They will, if the listener or reader responds to them with faith and in faith. The faith called for from adult men and women today is alert, inquiring, increasingly informed and educated. For as heirs of both our religious and our cultural heritages, we have a task: to build and rebuild the human order in our societies. There are other tasks in our world, many of them urgent. But hardly any other task has the pivotal or strategic significance that this one has.

The task is not limited to Christians, but Christians will be indispensable to it. Just as the world needs the Church for this task, the world and the Church alike need us. They need men and women committed to the human good in and on behalf of our societies, genuinely committed, and committed for the long haul.

The five speeches in Matthew induct the listener/reader into an atmosphere essentially created by Jesus. It is one of *faith, hope, and love.* These are *supernatural virtues, but faith, hope, and love are not misdirected but allowed their fullest scope when made to include and enhance our lives in the world.

In powerful ways, albeit in fragmentary form, the Sermon on the Mount has already impinged on the world through countless readers. Above we mentioned Mohandas Gandhi and Martin Luther King merely as two among conspicuous examples. We should certainly not allow their conspicuous example to excuse or discourage us from opening ourselves to the impact of these five great speeches, with a view to making what contribution we can to the sanity, health, well-being, and hope of the societies in which we live.

History is a compound of progress and decline. If we are to be on the side of progress, it will be through whatever human and religious authenticity the grace of God can effect in us. Jesus surely meant something along these lines when he invited us into "a better righteousness" so as to bring light to the world.

NOTES

1. Rudolf Pesch, "Levi-Matthäus (Mc 2,14/Mt 9,9; 10,3. Ein Beitrag zur Lösung eines alten Problems," *Zeitschrift für die neutestamentliche Wissenschaft* 59 (1968) 40–56.

2. Joseph A. Fitzmyer, "Aramaic *Kêphā'* and Peter's Name in the New Testament," in *Text and Interpretation*, Matthew Black Festschrift, ed. Ernest Best and R. M. Wilson (Cambridge: Cambridge University Press, 1979) 121–132. Reprinted in Fitzmyer, *To Advance the Gospel* (New York: Crossroad, 1981) 112–124.

3. Jacques Dupont, *Les Béatitudes*, 3 vols. (Louvain: Nauwelaerts, 2nd ed. 1958–63) Vol 1.

4. Gerd Theissen, "Jesusbewegung als charismatische Wertrevolution," *New Testament Studies* 35 (1989) 343–360.

5. Paul Gaechter, *Das Matthäus Evangelium. Ein Kommentar* (Innsbruck: Tyrolia, 1963).

6. David Wenham, "The Structure of Matthew XIII," *New Testament Studies* 25 (1978–79) 516–522.

7. Søren Kierkegaard, *Philosophical Fragments, or A Fragment of Philosophy*, by Johannes Climacus (Copenhagen, 1844). Trans. D. F. Swenson, rev. H. V. Hong (Princeton: Princeton University Press, 1967).

8. Bernard Lonergan, "The Future of Christianity," in Lonergan, *A Second Collection*, ed. W.F.J. Ryan and B. J. Tyrrell (Philadelphia: Westminster, 1974) 149–163, at 154–155.

GLOSSARY

Apocalypse: A literary genre that entered Jewish tradition ca. the third century B.C. It is represented in the Bible by chapters 24–27 in Isaiah, chapters 7–12 in Daniel, the Apocalypse of St. John in the New Testament. Apocalypticism is the movement that produced apocalyptic literature. Its key contribution to the biblical tradition, including John the Baptist and Jesus, was the radicalization of eschatology. See *Eschatological.*

Augustine, Saint (354–430): Bishop of Hippo in North Africa, who called on the parable of the tares amid the wheat to defend the Catholic view of the Church as including saints and sinners against the Donatists, who insisted on a Church of saints only, "the pure," who refused to coexist with "the impure."

Canonical: Belonging to the "canon," or list of inspired books. "Canonical Matthew" is the final Greek version of Matthew's Gospel, as distinct from any versions that might have existed prior to it.

Catchword Composition: A linking of short units on the mere basis of their having a word or phrase in common. It is often used in oral tradition as a memory device. Mark 9:49-50 links three disparate sayings on the basis of the word "salt": "For everyone will be salted with fire. Salt is good, but if salt has become insipid, how can you restore its tang? Have salt in yourselves and be at peace with one another."

Cosmopolis: A name for the informal international fraternity/sorority of the cultured. Civilized people count on this cultural elite to ridicule the pretentious, dismiss the tawdry, and support the authentic in thought, art, letters.

Divine Passive:　A mode of reverential circumlocution. The passive voice is used so as not to name God as subject of the verb, e.g. "happy those in mourning, for they *shall be comforted.*" (God will comfort them.)

Eschatological:　Pertaining to the climactic and decisive saving act of God. Once apocalypticism (see *Apocalyptic*) brought in the notion of God's absolutely climactic and definitive saving act, including a resurrection of the dead, Last Judgment, and Reign of God, eschatology became a transformer of biblical themes: Law and covenant, election and prophecy, "the righteousness of God."

Hegelian:　Pertaining to the philosophy of Georg Wilhelm Friedrich Hegel (1770–1831). What Kierkegaard especially opposed in Hegel was his identification of the content of religion and philosophy—in Kierkegaard's view, a reductionist cheapening of revelation and faith.

Josephus, Flavius:　Jewish historian of the first Christian century, whose masterpiece, *The Jewish War*, recounted the revolt (66–72/73) against Rome.

Kerygma:　The act and content of early Christian preaching. Its central theme was the act of God, on behalf of every human being, in the death and resurrection of Jesus, made Christ and Lord.

Kierkegaard, Søren (1813–1855):　Danish theologian and writer. His acute feel for the concrete structures of human existence, and for how the heritage of faith penetrates and enhances them, made him an incisive critic of efforts to "modernize" Christian faith.

Koine:　The Greek language as commonly spoken and written in eastern Mediterranean lands in the Hellenistic and Roman periods.

Ordeal/Tribulation:　In Old Testament texts a "time of affliction/tribulation" that was to precede the end. The Gospels refer to this by the Greek term *peirasmos* ("temptation," "ordeal," "trial"). Jesus himself understood that it would be launched by his own suffering and death. In the eschatological discourse (Matt 24:1–25:46) it is postponed to an indefinite future.

Parallelism:　Composition in which two (sometimes three) lines or half-lines have approximately equivalent rhythms and lengths. When the sense factor is added, distinct kinds of parallelism can be distinguished (synonymous, antithetic, climactic, etc.).

Parousia: The second coming of Christ at the end of time. The disciples inherited from Jesus a charged hope and expectation: "the day of the Son of Man," which would include Jesus' resurrection, his messianic enthronement, and his return on the clouds to judge the world. They found themselves compelled by events, however, to distinguish between "resurrection" (which happened on the third day following Jesus' death and included his messianic enthronement) and "parousia," his still future "second coming."

Philo of Alexandria: Greek-speaking and Greek-writing Jewish public figure and philosopher from Alexandria in Egypt, active in the first half of the first Christian century.

Proto-Luke: A hypothetical stage in the coming-to-be of the Gospel of Luke. According to the hypothesis, Proto-Luke included two currents of tradition: the special Lukan source and Q. It did not yet include Markan material.

Q Hypothesis: The view that material that is parallel in Matthew and Luke but lacking in Mark made up a single current of tradition. It consisted of sayings in Aramaic, translated early into Greek, and current orally in two versions: one now in Matthew, the other in Luke. In good part the sayings in our five speeches are from Q.

Redaction/Redactor: Edition/editor. The materials of the Gospels took shape first in oral form, as pre-literary sequences of tradition. When finally put in writing, they were edited, or redacted, to make a complete narrative. (Scholars differ widely on how much the variations among the Gospels are due respectively to oral tradition and to the written redactions.)

School of Alexandria: A school of biblical interpretation and theology whose leaders included Clement of Alexandria, Origen, and Cyril of Alexandria. Open to philosophy and religious speculation, the school was known for its "high" doctrine of Christ and for its allegorical interpretations.

Self-transcendence: The "going beyond" self and self-centered limitations in affection, love, knowledge, virtue. The result of this "going beyond" mere subjectivity is arrival at "authentic subjectivity." Self-transcendence is accordingly a key to fulfillment and happiness for the individual and to progress for society.

Sitz im Leben ("Setting in Life"): A recurrent social situation in which oral forms of Gospel tradition took shape. The liturgical act of celebrating the Eucharist, for example, helped to shape the Eucharistic words as recorded in the Gospels. (It does not follow that the Last Supper did not actually take place.)

Source Criticism/Source-Critical: The effort to trace the genesis of texts. This often includes relative dating. Supposing that our Gospels of Matthew, Mark, and Luke arose interdependently, source critics try to pin this down. Was Mark first? Did the others depend on him? Or was he last, and did he synthesize the others?

Stereotypic Feature (of Form): The oral form "miracle story" regularly exhibits traits such as: *introduction* (X comes forward); *request* ("Lord, if you will, you can make me clean"); *response* ("I will; be clean"); *conclusion* (instantly his leprosy was cleansed). These "traits" are stereotypes. Reaction of the crowd to a miracle is likewise a stereotypic feature of many miracle stories.

Supernatural: There are two uses of this term, one classical, the other popular. The classical use refers to the disproportion between "grace" and "nature" (grace enhances nature but is not reducible to nature). The popular use refers to the miraculous, sometimes categorized as "(scientifically) unexplained." In the present text the word is used only in the classical sense.

Symbolic Action: Jesus often placed acts that not only aimed at affecting concrete situations but also at projecting further meaning. Thus, cures and exorcisms not only helped the afflicted, but they also revealed the sense of Jesus' mission: how it related to Israel and what it meant for the power of Satan. The same held for his initiatives (e.g., table fellowship) toward notorious sinners, his choosing twelve special assistants (the number evoked the twelve tribes of Israel to be restored). The entry into Jerusalem, the cleansing of the temple, the Last Supper—all were charged with symbolic action and, like Jesus' words, appealed for faith.

Synoptic Gospels: The Gospels of Matthew, Mark, and Luke, called "synoptic" inasmuch as their many parallels can be lined up and taken in at one look (*opsis*). John's Gospel thus stands apart, despite its many basic bonds with the other Gospels.

Synoptic Question/Problem: In what sequence and with what relations of dependence did the Synoptic Gospels come into being? See *Source Criticism/Source-Critical.*

Synoptic Tradition: The sum of the traditions that entered the Synoptic Gospels. Inasmuch as the redactors/editors contributed not the content but the organization of their literary works, the historical worth of the Synoptic Gospels depends on the historical worth of the tradition.

Utopia/Utopianism: the word *Utopia* (Greek for "Nowhere") was invented by Thomas More as the name of an imaginary country. In a broader sense the term has come to signify visionary schemes for society. Though Karl Marx contemptuously denounced the social schemes of his competitors as utopian, his own schemes were equally fanciful and catastrophic for the peoples on whom they were tried.